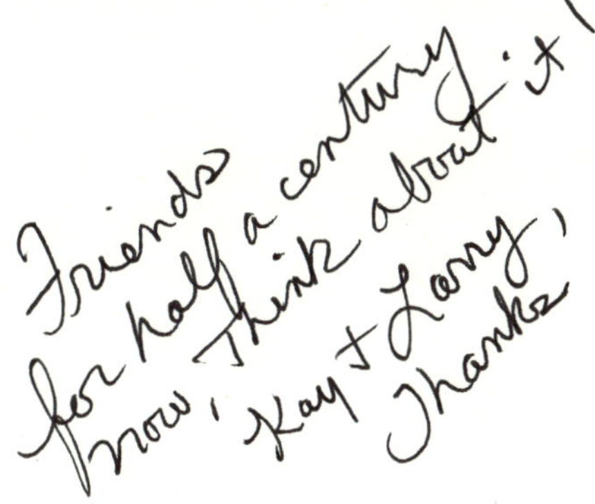

A Japanese Journey

Alone in the Land of the Rising Sun

P. Amalie Turner

Hitoride Press
Redmond, OR

A JAPANESE JOURNEY:
Alone in the Land of the Rising Sun

Hitoride Press
www.hitoridepress.com

Cover Design by Debra Turner
www.dtdesign.com

Shodo on page 12 created by Joe Fichter.
Poetry, haiku, and all other artwork throughout created by the author.

Editing & Book Production by Eva Long
evalong@comcast.net

Publisher's Cataloging-in-Publication
(Provided by Quality Books, Inc.)

Turner, P. Amalie.
A Japanese journey : alone in the land of the rising sun / P. Amalie Turner.
p. cm.
Includes index.
ISBN-13: 978-1-60725-477-5
ISBN-10: 1-60725-477-8

1. Turner, P. Amalie--Anecdotes. 2. Teachers, Foreign--Japan--Anecdotes. 3. Japan--Social life and customs--21st century--Anecdotes. 4. Japan--Description and travel. I. Title.

DS822.5.T87 2008 952.05
QBI08-600325

Printed in the United States of America

to

the Iwamotos

~ Akira, Tsuneko, and Akitoshi ~

Acknowledgments

My father, John Richard Turner,
for the gift of work ethic, survival instinct,
keen sense of direction,
and the value of a good education

My wonderful friends on Cape Cod,
at Brooks Library, Harwich, Writers Roundtable,
for encouraging me to dust off this manuscript
John Prophet, our mentor

My dear sister,
Debra Lynne Turner,
for a lovely cover design and two decades
of support, encouragement, and love

Rod Collins, WSU class of '60,
my gifted writer friend,
for finding me…out in the forest,
and setting my compass straight

Eva Long,
my precious and tactful editor,
who taught me
to throw out the whine
and take on the dream!
Her shepherding me for nearly a year now
has become a rare friendship.

Contents

Prologue ~ *9*

Alone ~ *13*

So, Let's Go! ~ *23*

Little Village Beyond the River ~ *29*

This is My Gotanno ~ *35*

The Children, I Can't Forget the Children ~ *42*

Common Sense: Overload! ~ *49*

The Iwamotos — My Wonderful Friends ~ *55*

Earthquake! And Fear of the Fathers ~ *68*

Kyoto, Calm and Quiet Walking Stones ~ 72

Somehow I Missed Kamogawa! ~ *80*

Iniri Kite Festival ~ *84*

Shopping! But What is It? ~ *90*

Take With You What You Cannot Do Without ~ *96*

The Mystery of the Mothballs ~ *101*

Wakayama, Set Sail! ~ *105*

Wakayama Homecoming ~ *109*

Nara: Ancient Times Recounted ~ *115*

Ancient of Ancestors ~ *124*

Reverent Silence Under Koya's Cedars ~ *129*

Naka-Meguro: The Other End of the Hibya Line ~ *134*

Darts & Hearts ~ *146*

Nikko: Shrine Extraordinary! ~ *158*

Hiroshima is a Feeling ~ *164*

Okutama: Chuo's End-of-the-Line ~ *168*

Matsumoto: Great Black Castle ~ *174*

Spring Sayonara Tears ~ *178*

Epilogue ~ *183*

Prologue

One May night,
I was unknowingly
Let free of a smothering chrysalis!
I felt my wings sticky with misgivings,
Wet with nervousness,
Stiff with mild fear
Of the unknown,
Trembling with an uncertain but sobering excitement.

In the bluish reflections of the Carson nightly monologue, I sat, propped up in bed, and continued scribbling on my "reasons" sheet. My fingers flew far behind my mind, the writing was surprisingly legible, and the left-hand "reasons to go" column filled up in no time.

I struggled with the "reasons to stay" column, perhaps in succinct delusion of self. I felt a midnight surge of old grief and fear echoing a newfound battle cry to reinvent myself. I had little to lose except the cost of those first three months abroad on a tourist visa, but everything to gain facing a challenge that had nothing to do with being part of a spouse, team, couple or pair!

It was me against the ocean that would lead me to my Japan.
Tonight, I thought, whether I knew it or not,
I had made one of the biggest decisions of my entire life.

I wrote this book to simply share the unequivocal daily joys I felt as an innocent bystander, a people-watcher, and an active participant in the everyday urban-suburban life of Japan.

I went to Japan on a three-month tourist visa.

I had finances to keep me afloat for three weeks!

And I stayed for three years.

My senses as a poet, writer, teacher, traveler, extrovert, friend, and artist were romanced in what became a true love affair—heart and mind—with Japan and its people.

I hope that I may touch the reader's heart with the warmth and adventures, the kindnesses and generosities offered to me by the wonderful people of Japan, who opened their hearts, homes, minds, and gardens to me, a wandering *geijin* (foreigner).

I traveled to places known to very few Americans and immersed myself in the vast profusion of customs and traditional fetes accorded few visitors.

I offer this book, meant to be a simple, personal travel memoir, to those who have held a hidden dream in their heart of hearts, and have not yet made their journey.

And I share it with those who have.

Domo arigato gozaimasu

P. Amalia Turner

Sapporo
Nagano
Toyama
Gifu
Kanazawa
Fukui
Ōtsu
Kyōto
Kōbe
Tottori
Okayama
Hiroshima
Fukuoka
Akita
Yamagata
Niigata
Sado Island
Aomori
Okutama
Morioka
Iniri
Sen'dai
Matsumoto
Fukushima
Nikko
Utsunomiya
Mito
Maebashi
Tōkyō
Chiba
Urawa
Kawasaki
Yokohama
Kamogawa
Kamakura
Shizuoka
Nagoya
Nara
Ōsaka
Wakayama

Japan

***Hitoride**:*

...alone, by oneself, voluntarily, spontaneously...

Hitoride

Alone

...halfway through the boarding tunnel, my knees locked,
my breath literally sucked out of me, and my mind screamed,
"You are leaving for what might become a very long time!"

Ask my brother-in-law, Paul. He said I was running from the reality of my catastrophic bankruptcy surrounding John's death. He was right. Enduring the remaining five years of my seven-year bankruptcy would be like riding the tail of a late fall hurricane. Couldn't even buy a lounge chair on layaway, let alone own a decent car. Widowhood stunk and destitution was not far behind.

Ask my children, Robyn, Bryan, and Kari. They had lost their father to a massive coronary eight years ago. I was forever, now, their only parent. Clearly, they did not want me leaving town, much less venturing out some four thousand five hundred and seventy-two miles away.

Ask me, why don't you? I needed air. I needed to process. Years and years worrying about my children's juvenile diabetes, years spent being a devoted but fierce warrior on their behalf, and years of major medical expenses still owed for their care had taken a toll.

I was not bailing out of my financial obligations; I just wouldn't. I dreamed that the fine wages in the Japanese teaching market could be mine and would allow me to wire money home to my family and put those enormous stacks of bills behind me. This was hard to do on a single teacher's salary in Brothers, Oregon, and this salary was now in jeopardy since the local school board was dead set against giving me tenure for a third year in their little red, one-room schoolhouse on the high desert.

I was exhausted and numb with loneliness. Facing the enormity of relocation to yet a new community and making new friends made the idea of getting away even easier. The health of my married twenty-four-year-old Robyn was stabilized, twenty-one-year-old Bryan was now a newlywed, and twenty-year-old Kari had just enrolled in the state university. I now came to a very clear and startling realization: Things just seemed to be lining up for me to pack up and pack out in a direction I choose!

And so, I thought, "If I have to reinvent myself and a new identity, I shall go abroad and fulfill a childhood dream."

When, if not now?

A self-avowed, fierce, native Oregonian, I was born in the early 1940s in downtown Portland on the same block, with the same neighbors, and same elementary school teachers as my mother. We happy Norwegians just never got off Forty-Ninth and Taylor for sixty years, and it was here I was surrounded by aunties and uncles and *nana*s and *bonka*s and a plethora of step-cousins.

But at eighteen I couldn't wait to hasten off to the valley's teachers college, where I plowed through honors courses with gusto. Five years later I walked across the stage six months pregnant to receive my bachelor of science degree in elementary education. John, my Michigan State husband, followed me two years later, switching from forestry to earn his B.A. in elementary education at Southern Oregon in Ashland.

For the next thirteen years we made a colorful couple, teaching in remote rural schools, and raising three delightful little "sagebrush" redheads on the Oregon high desert, east of the mighty Cascades.

When John went out jogging that June morning, days short of his 38th birthday, we had just realized a short-term dream of opening our own glass and mirror shop and getting out of education. His aortic explosion that day plunged the children and me into an exacerbated, catastrophic bankruptcy, and years of mourning.

So here I was, then, eight short years later, on a fine spring evening, facing both termination from an utterly romantic, idyllic, frontier-setting classroom of twelve students, K-8, and the not-so-romantic reality of my financial situation. Here I sat, wanting to create a childhood dream, avoid severe empty nest syndrome, and justify not just leaving town, but leaving the United States as well.

Three months later, with the little school-on-the-prairie now locked up, my son, Bryan, had come to the back door of my rental bungalow. I was practicing eating lunch with my first set of *ohashi* and feeling very awkward in the silence of getting caught at it. He handed me my mail but held back a familiar brown government envelope, return address "Passport Agency, Seattle, Washington," which he waved in the air deliriously.

With pain in his voice, he blurted, "You're really going to do it, aren't you? I can't believe you're going to do it!" And with hot tears running down his cheeks, he turned and left as quickly as he'd come.

I sat there, my heart breaking quietly for both of us. *But you've always wanted to go to Japan,* my voice niggled at me softly, *ever since you were twelve and your teacher tagged you gifted and talented at Glencoe Grade School in Portland. Dad and Mom somehow found the money to send you to Junior Art Museum in the west hills of the famed City of Roses during your fifth-grade summer. There you were, splashing through watercolor washes of majestic Mt. Fuji in thirteen different shades and perspectives, and attempting calligraphy—called* shodo—*with a gusto unmerited by its results. Japan, in your vocabulary, was hidden in your twelve-year-old heart of dreams.*

Diary entry: *Tokyo, 24th day, 8th month, year of the Emperor 1989. I woke just before dawn in Seattle. Today I have experienced 21 hours of daylight as we flew, arching first over Alaska, then the blue Pacific, then east to Asia, chasing the sunset which would set for me some 24 hours later. The "by myself" was replaced with a strange sense of power and confidence, and I am grateful anxiety has been replaced with keen anticipation.*

I was grateful to have this anticipation, for halfway through the boarding tunnel back in Seattle, my knees had locked, my breath had been literally sucked out of me, and my mind had screamed, *You are leaving for what might be a very long time!*

For the first time in six weeks it became so very real to me and I was shocked. On August 24, 1989, at 1:15 PST, I felt that I was stepping through a time portal, or like walking through a brick wall. At 1:15 PST, I was truly leaving.

And now I was approaching the land of my dreams. It was a foggy, lingering dusky evening when we touched down at Narita International Airport, through heavy gray-black clouds of the day's late August rain. I saw a patchwork of concrete power poles, miles of rice paddies, blue tile roofs on wonderful two-story, box-like homes. As the ground rushed at me, I was flooded with images of what I had hoped Japan to be—rinsed clean, wet, and brilliant in the early dusk. So this was Japan!

And here I was, *hitoride*—alone.

I must have looked vulnerable and very bewildered, for Customs waved me through and immigration lines had taken only forty-five minutes. After nearly twelve hours in the air, it felt great to stand and stretch. The huge Narita lobby was punctuated with twelve long lines of weary travelers coming in all at once from foreign flights from all corners of the world. All of us were converging on Tokyo, the second largest city in the world, with its inadequate system of screaming taxis and underground trains ready to lumber us into her core. The megalopolis city was still nearly ninety minutes away from this hub of exhausted aliens, all of us longing for food and shelter in the long day's night.

In Seattle, my suitcase on wheels had weighed in at one hundred and fifty pounds, and now a searing pain gripped my chest and made the heavy, damp island air very hard to breathe. Just yesterday, while putting the storage unit lock on my earthly possessions, my mother's antique piano stool had plummeted from high atop some kitchen crates. Hands full and unable to catch it, I took a hard hit on my sternum; I remembered that sharp and quick crack. Now, while putting my carry-on luggage in the overhead compartment halfway over the Pacific, the alarming sensation returned to my chest and became, what I would later learn, a severely fractured rib. This would plague me and daunt my physical well-being for many weeks to come.

Having read countless books on travel in Japan that short summer, I had absolutely no knowledge of the Japanese language save seven cursory, stilted phrases of survival: *Oh hi yo go zai mus* (good morning), *co knee chee wah* (good afternoon), *con bon wah* (good evening), *ah ree gah toe* (thank you), *dough zo* (please); *toy ray* (restroom), *eki* (train station). And *oh do ku desuka* (where is it?)—this one became my favorite.

I at least had acquired the travel savvy to have phoned ahead for a week at the Ichigaya YWCA for a spartan room, no board, and had made calls to my new home church, St. Paul's International Lutheran, and the highly revered Pastor Carl Westby, who graciously offered to send a volunteer youth missionary out to the airport to welcome and escort me "into the city."

I had never met this man, but I had consulted the Lutheran Church Missouri Synod Directory and called the only Lutheran church in all of Tokyo. Pastor Westby cheerfully agreed to send a proper party to escort me safely into his beloved city of some twenty-four years. He had the enviable reputation of being the most Japanese-speaking pastor on the entire island of Honshu, and he and his congregation wrapped their welcoming and loving and hospitable arms around me from the first hour I set foot on the archipelago capital. This is the Lutheran way!

It would be many hours before I could put down my lumbering and inhuman Samsonite companion with its two unsteady back wheels. Like a faithful puppy, I followed Karla, my volunteer youth escort, dragging this dreadful brown monster. Every painful step—from airport to bus, bus to escalator, escalator to the train tracks, through electric doors, up miles of mountains of steep and narrow Tokyo stairways—reminded me of my mother's piano stool.

Once in the city, Karla handed me off to Priscilla, the prim, Canadian church-missionary secretary, who led me through the next phase, the mega-station of Shinjuku, then finally to the Ichigaya YWCA where I was so gratefully pre-registered. It was easy to wave off her hospitality with my staggering fatigue *cum laude* and anticipate some much-needed sleep.

As soon as Priscilla left, however, I followed the steps of what would be my first of many relaxing Japanese *ofuro,* a bathing ritual begun by first showering away impurities, then soaking the spirit and soul in a huge square tub until shriveled or fried, whichever comes first.

In bed at last in this stark and convent-like room with darkened shades, sleep came fitfully. There weren't enough pillows to hug my angry rib cage, so I contented myself to sleep propped up against the stucco wall, while neon-blitzed overloads of the teeming city from elevated train tracks whizzed across my eyelids in crisp reruns. The clanking of train tracks and *gettas* (sandals) tapping on glassy concrete station floors kept knocking on my eardrums.

My body was so caught up in the sensual overload of my new city that I could hardly sleep. Beyond fatigue and into disbelief I passed a very short night, a pathetic figure of unrest. Still, I was here! But I was hurting. And I was alone.

Next morning at seven, I woke and stirred, riddled with hunger. At thirty-five dollars a night I was determined to get my money's worth, so I took still another quick shower in the quaint *tatami*-mat bathing room, dressed, and was out on the street by eight-thirty. The morning was hot, muggy, and very overcast, like a day after a forest fire when the smoke hangs at eye level—an eerie reddish yellow. I found a wonderful *soba* noodle shop just three blocks away at Iidabashi Station on the murky canal. Purchasing one quick vending machine ticket, I joined fellow "slurpers" at the stand-up counter.

I came away completely revitalized by the rich, steamy broth and whole-wheat noodles, and this was to become the regular sum and substance of my diet as the Japanese economy would quickly eat huge holes in my financial resources. Day one's trains, buses, meals, and motel came to nearly one hundred and thirty-three dollars. If I don't get a job soon, I won't last ten days!

So this was the land of neon and cranes, nightlife and fast trains, in daylight and late summer, eh? Now in late August the autumn monsoons had already begun, and in my five-hour walk I got soaked to the skin and had to buy an umbrella. Caught up in the brisk walking traffic, I clutched at myself to ease my jarring ribs and envisioned shredding the hotel sheets to bind myself as my mother, a victim of pleurisy, had done.

Yet by seven that night, I had visited nearby Kitanomaru Park, found the Lutheran Center and met my beloved Pastor Westby, mastered the above-ground, color-coded train system, and ventured to Akihabara, the electric city and "Sony shopping center of the world." I had done the famous Yamanote Loop—a sixty-five-minute ride around this famed city, at rush hour no less, and for less than a dollar! What a deal!

Having eaten nothing more the rest of that day than a banana and bottled water, I celebrated my triumphant adventure with a hearty evening meal at a wonderful second-story terrace restaurant. By simply pointing to the owner's plastic reproductions in the showcase, I was able to order beef vegetables, chow mein, rice, soup, tofu, and a large Kirin beer, then wolf them down while the natives marveled at my chopstick expertise—by staring discreetly as only the Japanese can.

Watching the teeming world below, I observed that a five-way intersection around the neighborhood *koban* (police box) can be a veritable three-ring circus. Early evening drunks dodging madmen taxi drivers, and successful young Japanese working women, juggling parcels from an all-day shopping spree, dashing on spike heels over six-lane boulevards to beat the traffic lights can make for some pretty exciting, wide-screen spectating. Since people-watching has always been a hobby of mine, I see that I have come to the right place. Definitely.

I once more indulged in the Japanese shower-then-soak ritual, and somehow this night, sleep overtook my pain—eleven hours of deep, merciful sleep.

Diary Entry: *"Had a great first day out today. People do not stare, and I would not care. And I am far from tall, for I had been led to believe we Americans were so much taller in stature and I was prepared to stand out a bit.*

Not so, ahhh so, here in the Land of the Rising Sun…today was full of many wonderful surprises.

Today, I really do not feel hitoride.

I am in love with Tokyo already!

~

If a glimpse through the clouds
of a days gentle thunderstorm
was a capsule of Japan–
then rice fields
and blue tile roofs
and electric towers,
tiny white work trucks
and narrow roads
punctuating bamboo forests
would be a truth!

~

E-to, Ikimasho!

So, Let's Go!

The truth was: In my heart of hearts,
I knew there was a job in Japan with my name on it.

My first Sabbath in a Shinto Buddhist land greeted me with yet more rain. This was humbling because, as a fiercely-proud, native Oregonian, I thought I knew "rain." The view outside my second-story room at the YWCA told me otherwise: This was a veritable white-out. Since I had yet to see the sun, I was already having a hard time getting my bearings here.

With this fierce pain still raging in my chest, how would I wrestle the famed rolling behemoth over wet cobbles to the storage room at my new Lutheran church home? Sporting my flashy, hot pink Meier & Frank raincoat, I struck out and allowed myself plenty of time. Along the side street of the winding canal, I noted handsome hotels and coffee shops, and the welcome shelter from the downpour of thick, old cherry trees lined up like short, stubby soldiers. Will these leaves turn color in the autumn? Already I am anxious for September and a new season.

At St. Paul's International Lutheran Church near Ichigaya Station, one of the kind ushers offered to take my suitcase to the mission storage room on the second floor. I found the women's restroom clearly marked "toi-ray" and removed my coat. What met me in the mirror was a horrifying sight! I was soaked to my skin, through three layers of clothing, including blouse and slip. I stripped down and dried myself under the wall-mounted hand dryer as best I could. The congregation was well into the liturgy by the time I arrived at the sanctuary.

The combination of warm, penetrating rains, plus Sunday's one hundred percent humidity had not been kind to me, and there was more to come: Typhoon "Number Three" of the season hovered offshore and would hit us that night. I quickly learned that typhoons are not named as are hurricanes; they are merely numbered. A typical season might have seventeen, but "Number Three" was plenty for me in these early days of my Japanese life.

It's not merely by chance that I was able to make my way all over Tokyo my first weekend, like a caterpillar on a mission. From the time I applied for my passport back in Oregon, I had read every book on Japan in our county library and had purchased several myself. I loved the strange looks on the faces of the bookstore's staff when I asked them "anything you have on Japan?" Perhaps because of the size of my town, it was unique to strike out to this far eastern country—particularly in the summer, with possibly seventeen hurricanes to look forward to, a most hostile season for visitors.

More direct were the reactions from my church family and circle of lifetime friends to the news I was leaving for Japan: They thought I was totally out of my tree!

To strike out alone, with the minimum legal financial resources required by the Japanese government upon entry seemed pretty brassy and over-confident to most of my colleagues. Selling a great portion of my lifetime possessions at a spontaneous yard sale in late July was also very final. And putting what little I had left of my "stuff," as comedian George Carlin called it, into a rental storage unit ten-foot square could have communicated a decided message of my never returning again.

But I was here now, and it felt so right.

Surely, I thought, no one would actually count my Traveler's Checks when I entered the country on the standard, ninety-day tourist visa. No one would see how under-funded I really was, with nothing more than a six-day reservation at the local YWCA. I had resources for perhaps two to three weeks at most. Not even my children knew that.

While still in Oregon counting my days until departure, I had set to memorize the color-maze maps of each and every subway system and the amazing above-ground Japan Railways transit system, fondly known as the JRT. I visualized the tactics of getting on a train car packed to twice its normal capacity without getting "pushed" by polite conductors in their chin-strap caps and fresh white gloves. I memorized how to tumble off without falling down and being trampled alive by the very assertive and often combative Japanese on their way home—always late for somewhere.

I'd traveled all over Europe in 1964 and survived the French Metro and British subways, so I was sure the Japanese system operated on the same color and count theory. I was delightfully surprised to find the Japanese transportation system very user-friendly and hospitable to English speakers. Within Tokyo proper, most stations, just minutes apart in intervals, were labeled and subtitled in English, until you passed city limits—beyond the famous "Yamanote Loop", that is. That's when the challenge began and the adrenalin rushes took over.

I found the Japanese language with its Hiragana-Katakana phonetic base—(a)=ah, (e)=eh, (i)=ih, (o)=oh, (u)=oo—a real breeze to pronounce once I heard it or saw it in English. Once I had mastered the vowel systems and rules—that most vowels are short vowels, or schwas, and each short syllable has full pronunciation—things began to unlock for me. Tokyo: "toe-kyo," not "toe-kee-yo," as we are given to say. Narita: "nah-ree-tah," not "nair-eat-uh." Despite its brisk and clipped sounds, when one rolls r's as well as I could, I was soon impressing even the locals with my echolalia. This was very good for my morale and gave me a sense of settling in.

Now I was greeting the lovely, pale receptionist at the check-in desk of the "Y" politely submitting my key each time with a greeting like *ohayo gozaimasu* (good morning) and *kombanwa* (good evening).

Every day I was so pumped and caught up in the power surge of the people on the sidewalks that my circulation seemed to pick up the pace.

The Japanese always seemed to be on a dead run. Physically, they never touch nor bump into you; they just move in a personal gear of overdrive with an incredible sense of self and self-control. My new friend, Yoshi, later explained it to me this way: "If you live with a family of five in a space less than the average American living room year after year, and sleep at night on that floor on futons, racked up bum-to-bum, you learn to move in tight spaces with little or no true body contact."

So moving with the Japanese became an art. I felt like a dance student swallowing the beat. My body began to move in a lithe rhythm that allowed me to bend and dodge, yet never touch. I felt good. I felt right. This was appreciated.

On the other hand, it took me a while to automatically move down the correct side of the sidewalk. True to British form, the correct side was the left side, not the right. Afoot or on bicycles, one leads their body to the left. This alone took me several weeks to master.

Drive on the left, pass only on the right, and one stays on the left of the sidewalk when walking. (When I returned home to Oregon the following summer, afoot or behind the wheel, I was a menace for days getting reoriented.)

I was shaken into reality on my third day. As enjoyable and almost timeless as it felt to be able to soak in the people and their culture, the reality was that if I wanted to stay, I had to find work.

Here was the truth: In my heart of hearts, I knew there was a job in Japan with my name on it. When I finally faced job-hunting head on, I buoyed myself each day with four parts optimism, four parts good fortune, four parts qualifications for the jobs I knew were out there for certified language teachers, and finally four parts fierce energy—then added a truckload of prayers.

If employment could not be found, a disappointing Plan B would be to simply enjoy myself, spend every last dime I had, return on my round-trip ticket, and substitute teach the remainder of the year or perhaps fall into a job opening back home. I had pre-paid my car payments and insurances through the new year and I figured I could find a housemate while I got on my feet.

But late one afternoon, I called the employment agency I had registered with via mail, having already sent my credentials, updated resumé, and certified copy of my current Oregon teaching certificate in early August. The enthusiastic office manager at the other end of the line fairly shrieked, "Patricia, have we found a job for you!" I almost dropped to my knees, rubber as they were in the noisy little phone booth at "restaurant central," and, with incredulous joy, stared at the torrid pink plastic phone in my hand.

And so it would both amaze and astound me, that by day six I had an apartment, a job, a month's salary advance, and time left over to travel and soak up the sights and sounds of my exciting new country.

I was hopelessly enamored with this place and I knew it. That voice that got me here now said *Ikimasho*!—Let's get on with it!!

Kawa No Mukouno Chiisa Na Mura

Little Village Beyond the River

Haunted, hallowed and lonesome cemeteries
cradling ancestors under stark, lonely, but well-chosen trees...
trails of freshly lit incense sticks being lifted heavenward
by the subtle afternoon breezes...

On my second Monday in this new land I would at last meet with my sponsors, the Lowerys, visit my village, and see the school that was to become my home. I was going to Gottano.

In order to stay beyond my tourist visa and teach in Japan, the government would ask for a "letter of guarantee" from a resident, assuring the country that you are financially sound; that they will pay your living and transportation. You must show a graduation certificate, write your personal history, submit passport-size photos, and be prepared to leave the country and re-enter formally as a registered Alien Citizen.

When Jon Lowery rapturously gushed that he had seen my credentials, that he was sure I was the person for the job, that I must come out as quickly as possible to see the new school, meet his family, and that he was sure "the children would love me!!", visions of Anna in "Anna and the King" danced in my head as my heart sang "the children, the children, I can't forget the children."

To come to Japan and teach English as a second language to precious little pie-faced, doe-eyed Japanese toddlers was the fulfillment of a dream.

I remember asking Jon questions like, "How far out is Gottano? How big a village is it? What are the living conditions?" to which he answered a prosaic "...no one knows quite where Tokyo ends and Saitama Prefecture begins, but it's a small town and you will have a fine apartment up over the school."

Once more, visions of life in a quaint, fishing village overlooking the ancient Edo River, putrid with its fishing stench, and a fine view of majestic Mt. Fuji nearly one hundred miles away from my sliding rice paper shutters thrilled me in anticipation. In my vision I would go to the rooftop to hang laundry and worship this real-life image every day to enlighten my soul. The children would flock to lessons in their little bare feet and padded kimono tops and sit gazing up at me, the new *sensai*, Pat-o-san!

So when I took the Hibya Line train north to Tahkenotsuka to be wined, dined, and enrolled by the Lowery family as *sensai*-in-chief of their fine new Gottano English School, I motored through the time warp that engulfs Tokyo proper and separates this throbbing metropolis from the Japan that has always been and might ever be—simply by slipping out over the Edo River.

One has only to travel at these high speeds on the spotless, aluminum turbo-train cars to be propelled into "VistaVision" settings of ancient, rural Edo history—farmers bent to the land in the manual labor of planting, tilling, harvesting, nurturing, and honoring—generation after generation on the same plots their centuries of ancestors had in turn planted, tilled, harvested, nurtured, and loved.

This reverence was reflected in manicured, picturesque scenes—spotless showcase homes, valiant and proud, dotting the landscape, many elevated on small plots to escape spring rains and temporary lakes created by monsoons and the merciless torrents that come down from the highlands.

I saw the haunted, hallowed, and lonesome cemeteries cradling ancestors under stark and lonely but well-chosen trees, trails of freshly lit incense sticks being lifted heaven-ward by the subtle afternoon breezes.

I saw handsome outbuildings with red or cobalt blue tile roofs as splendid as the family mansion, storage for crude plows sitting side-by-side with the most recent model of a John Deere or Kubota tractor. I saw rice winnows, rakes, and scythes leaning against a hand-set rock wall perhaps a thousand years old in a land that was aready two thousand years old when my own country was suffering its birthing pains.

This, then, was the Japan I had so long imagined. Whitewashed stucco walls of these sunbaked old buildings spoke to me of the battles on the plains between shogun war lords and warring Japanese tribes. Out of their bloodshed came the land law that every surviving family may have its meager forty or eighty acres to support their family, 'til death do them all part. Now, the last two generations have scoffed at the land and dirty hands, and have gone off to the nearby cities to seek their computer-age fortune, leaving their fathers and ancient crafts, foregoing their inheritances to pioneer their lives in the big urban areas and even bigger countries of the world, some never returning.

Still, tradition does exist. Honor to ancient fathers and traditions occurs only when son takes a bride and brings her home to show her off. If the eldest son and heir so chooses, the dynasty goes to the next son down, or may pass, with the fortune, to the husband of a daughter who, in that case, must take her family name when he marries.

I am impressed with the manicured miles of onions and iris, rice and sweet potatoes, peanuts and spinach, and wonder where the next generation of tillers and harvesters will come from, for in order to continue Japan's farm-to-market economy, foreign laborers will soon have to be imported, or this too will die. I am saddened by this fact, and I walk quietly and let those walls speak to me.

Already, in the area north of Tokyo near the "Science City" of Tskuba, hundreds of acres of prime rich soil have fallen victim to the rock crushers at the foot of nearby Mt. Tskuba, and urban sprawl in the form of a Disney-like, futuristic city that has sprung up out of the rice hulls to welcome a population of nearly a quarter of a million "juppies," or Japan urban professionals. Their fine Tskuba University is host to some of the latest technology, world science forums, and research laboratories of Japan's future.

I shake myself from my daydreaming, gather my things, and detrain for my formal introduction to my very British professor-employer.

Through the ticket turnstile, a beaming, ruddy-faced Englishman awaits, a full six-foot-six. This is Jon Lowrey, my boss. Jon is the only foreigner in the whole village, but he, too, has married into wealth and taken the name, fame, and fortune of a lovely, British-educated native Japanese woman, Junko—"june-ko," the "ko" being the suffix for a girl child.

And it is here they have chosen to settle and raise their three young children.

I'm delighted to meet him and to have escaped the pace of Tokyo proper with an introduction to the early autumn landscape of greater rural Japan.

A brisk walk north of the humming train tracks takes us to their parcel, which was once, Jon tells me, a rice farm, of course, but is now a sprawling subdivision of pitiful, clone-like high-rise apartments, where the sounds of continued construction ring on into the night.

Now, a fairly informal interview by Jon and Junko takes place in a most formal office-den, where I am taken through my resumé with close scrutiny while I marvel at Junko's expertise and their very Oxford accents! My eyes wander to the glass showcase in the corner where a samurai breast-plate and helmet rest on a mannequin with a beastly, hairy, animal-like face resembling a badger. This, I am told, was the face that frightened even brave tribal warriors; it surely would me!

When my hosts have satisfied their curiosity about me, about my tenacity to come to Japan alone, and about my commitment to stay, they offer me what is truly a most generous contract: a furnished apartment, salary, and sponsorship into the country when my ninety-day tourist visa expires. They explain that only Junko, a native and landowner, can be my sponsor, so the paperwork will be tenuous, and I will be required to take a side trip to Seoul, Korea, in late November to be reprocessed into the country. But they agree to pick up those costs also and, in fact, offer a generous living allowance to cover my expenses while the facility was being completed.

I am very happy!

And now comes the ancient Japanese custom to celebrate such a coming-of-hire with a spontaneous party at the nearest local fish house. I feel sure this is the place and moment I am about to taste my very first *sushi, sashimi, sake*—"etcetera etcetera," as the King would say to Anna. I remember muttering, "Please God, don't let me throw up in front of a lot of people!"

The spontaneous party they threw that night was a hallmark for me. From the trains and nearby streets, pouring through the sliding rice paper door of this warm and wonderful dinner house, came half the village locals, nearly all of Lowery's closest friends. Word really spread fast in these parts.

In town for the Olympic trials that year was the Italian bicycle team of four, adding much color and laughter to the pub that night.

There were *sushi* rolls of every nature and description tumbling off the tiny bamboo mats behind the glass showcase. Mini-machetes were deftly splitting rolls of seaweed-wrapped rice cones, stuffed with asparagus, green beans, sauteed carrot slices, squid, octopus, tuna, kettle fish, sword fish, whale, and salmon, and all those new delicacies found their way to my little hand painted, ceramic plate for my first trial.

I drank hot *miso* soup made from soybean paste with tiny tofu squares floating on top amidst diced onion greens. This made my nose run. There were mountains of rice in wee ebony lacquered bowls. Order after order on thin platters came the raw fish, to be dipped in *wasabi*, a potent green horseradish that looked disarmingly like innocent guacamole, with the power of a nuclear payload and quite capable of choking you to death if you were unaware of its potency.

And I, as guest of honor, ate with my *ohashi* expertise, to the utter delight and amazement of the primarily male audience. They in turn were greatly entertained by my Yankee accent, yet made me feel so very welcome to their little village out beyond the great river.

I don't remember catching the train home that night, but I did. Nor did I remember the ninety-minute ride back into the belching whale stomach of the city.

Where, I was wondering as I made my way home, is Gottano, and the barefoot children?

Watashi No Machi Gotanno

This is My Gotanno

I will pile everything on shelves in this clever hideaway, under the stairs, and continue to live out of my suitcases.

Though the first-floor language school was "still under construction," and I would have until Tuesday, October 3, to get settled in, the apartment upstairs was ready, and Jon and Junko were quite excited for me to see it.

I had no trouble getting out of the city to Kita-Senju, the last English subtitled station, but from there over the river from the city proper, they said I should count carefully two stations and disembark at "Gotanno." *Go* in Japanese means "five," and I knew the character for the number five. Sure enough, as the electric doors of my sterile aluminum car flushed wide, the platform sign looked recognizably like a "go-tah-no," meaning "five rice fields."

But that's where the delusion ended.

I was but seven walking blocks from the pea-green, stenchy, ancient, tideless Edo river, and the dirt-packed streets I envisioned were but an extension of Tokyo. Once five rice fields, Gottano was in this century a veritable flourishing farm-to-market hub of sixty thousand affluent people in the Adachi-Ku, our equivalent of a county.

It was the home, therefore, of a stunning steel and glass municipal headquarters the likes of which I'd only seen in Houston! Trains rise out of the underground belly of Tokyo proper and surface once north beyond the Edo, rumbling along elevated tracks, clicking and clanking every two to three minutes, crissing and crossing overhead like unseasonal thunder from 5:00 a.m. promptly until exactly 12:47 a.m. the next morning—impeccable mass transit for nineteen hours and forty-seven minutes. My quaint, second floor *apato* (apartment) was but a brisk ninety seconds walk from the station.

So much for the barefoot children, I tell myself, in utter despair.

I was overwhelmed by the noise and thousands of people bustling about. The Lowerys were on the platform to meet me, and as we charged down the stairs and out onto the streets, it was like walking into a carnival at its height.

Under the tracks was a brand new McDonald's restaurant teeming with school children in their crisp navy and white military uniforms, uniforms that would simultaneously be changed to become black and white woolies on a designated day in late summer in a ritual called *koromogae*.

For now, though, the August heat and humidity has relegated us all to moist, sweaty pools, and it was traditional to carry a cotton hanky and daintily mop one's brow at regular intervals. I agonized for these young boys in their white shirts and dress ties; but they resembled any sea of happy teens feasting on fries and colas. I note the window signs: "All this for five hundred twenty yen," which was nearly four dollars.

The streets of Gottano are about a taxi and a half wide, such that passing cars must often take to the curbs. Heavy steel guard rails line the even more narrow sidewalks to prevent hourly fatalities, I was sure. The pedestrians, on a dead run to make trains or dinner deadlines, often take to the streets in what plays out as visible chaos and human foosball.

It's a scene of Japanese salarymen in traditional pea-green summer suits, playing dodge ball with bright yellow, red, and green and white cabs, with rare but occasional private vehicles playing the game too. All this was punctuated by hundreds of cyclists with their tinkle bell warnings ringing on their handle bars!

I suffer a brief visual overload of a two- to three-story stucco and tile town, laid out like the Pied Piper's Rottenburg hamlet in Germany, going this way and that with no two streets parallel, inhabited by sixty thousand new neighbors, most of whom I am convinced are on their way to town today and rushing to the station.

We three appear to be going against the traffic and tide this morning. Perhaps, I tell myself, we should stay off the streets until noon or after seven when the rush is over.

When I registered as an alien at one of the steel and glass palaces, the official map given me confirmed that there is no sanity to this town. Nothing is parallel, sensible, or dependable. Getting lost, and often, I could only listen for the trains overhead, make my way back to the station, and strike out again. I wondered how taxi cabs, ambulances, and surely the postal saints made their way through this mouse maze of humanity in a density ratio of one hundred seventy persons per one square block!

Junko's sister, Shizuko Kato, greeted me. A brusk, chain-smoking recent divorcée nearly my age, she was the owner of the Kato Building, home of the future J. L. English School, and of "Pah-to's new *apato*."

Located on the second floor, I faced the steepest flight of stairs I had ever seen in my entire life and it would be several weeks before I could get down them without manhandling the railing, especially with my still-painful ribs. To add to the challenge, the stairs were obviously not designed for the enormous feet of *geijin,* including my size ten and a half walking shoes. I was forced to step practically sideways.

The apartment was quite small. I had to duck to enter and Jon had to fold himself in. Junko and Shizuko, obviously devoted sisters who, at their diminutive four-foot-seven each and weighing less than a hundred pounds apiece, giggled in unison at my discomfort. Feeling like Alice in the Wonderhouse, I resigned myself to what it would take to get used to all of this.

Shizuko welcomed us on the tour with a pot of green Japanese tea as we knelt in the middle of my bare, new one-room home, nine by seventeen feet, auxiliary hallway with its toilet fit for an airplane in a bathroom containing a very small, square combo tub and shower stall. Later, I found my lone closet tucked in under the stairwell that led to the third floor, Shizuko's penthouse home.

But now, on the fresh but dusty hardwood floor, my new landlady raised her palm-sized cup in both hands and said in a well-rehearsed and obviously proud speech: "Welcome Pah-to-san, *sensai.*" I cried. I have a new and trusted friend, even if we shall never, ever speak the same language.

I gazed at high frosted windows, one per wall. I'm a claustrophobic, and my first thought was that in case of fire, no way would my Norwegian buttocks fit out and through them! No traditional, sliding rice paper screens, no view of Fuji-*san,* only the parking lot below for tenants of all the high rise apartments that now choke, smother, and block out the daylight. I am like Burton's "Little House," surrounded by asphalt and clamor. Daylight and sunrise shall escape me, and only on late summer days will I have a sense of sunset. For me now, the sun rises in the east over the Pacific and sets over the west on the shoulders of Mt. Fuji.

But now claustrophobia sets in immediately, compounded with the stark nakedness of white walls, metal kitchen cabinets, and steel sink. This is the room where I will eat and sleep and entertain, weather storms and experience earthquakes, and sit in darkness to hide from overwhelming but well-intentioned neighbors for the next ten months. If they see my lights on, they shall want what is left of me after my long workdays.

And never once would I see another *geijin* pass down my sidewalk to the station. I am an Anna, swallowed up in the immenseness of Tokyo rising from the ashes—no one knows quite where Tokyo ends and the prefectures, or counties, of rural Japan begin. And right at this moment, no one but God and my hosts knows where I am.

During the next three days I made my way to and from the city, moving from the YWCA, exiting the train, and afoot, dragging and hauling, huffing and puffing, two enormous suitcases and my heavy duty backpacks and shoulder bags, and all my Nippon-land earthly possessions to my wee little home at 1-3-25 Koudou, Adachi-ku. The postal system now becomes evident, and I am quite elated. I figured it out all by myself: first block from the station, third building in that block, twenty-fifth drop box…with, of course, the only *geijin* name in town, "Pah-toe-lee-she-uh Tul-neh," Patricia Turner, in a land with no "r" sound for surnames. I'm such an easy hit for my wonderful, ever-smiling mailman on his gutsy little white Kawasaki street bike, and we become fast friends.

A two-burner gas plate arrived as a welcome gift from my boss and his family right away. On my own, I purchased a toaster oven and my own refrigerator downtown at Electric City. I remember my state of excitement ordering it from a catalogue through the electric company, which would deliver it within three days. Until then, I had to either starve or eat out because by now the "dog-days of September" had set in, and it was very, very hot. Any foodstuff I might have bought would have readily spoiled, so I ate day-by-day and enjoyed the sidewalk-counter *soba* shops.

So sorry. An air conditioner, my employer explained, was simply not in the budget, so I would seek relief from the heat in the new classroom below or simply endure the torturously hot days.

When the *kuro reizuko*—the little black refrigerator—arrived, I was hopelessly excited. I didn't reckon that by Japanese standards, this horrid black, basically plastic box that ate up nearly $375 of my personal and remaining funds, would stand less than four feet tall and hold all of a quart of milk, two quart beers, hydrator vegetables and fruits, and a half dozen eggs. But it kept bread from turning green overnight in this foreign land of fungus and mold, and I found that the simple delights of ice cubes on an unbearable day, and having fresh or frozen pork chops were well worth the sacrifice. This little black box would follow me everywhere for the next three years and be my true and faithful friend. And when I sold it in June of 1992, I got seventy-five dollars for it.

So this is home—1-3-25, downtown Gottano, all two hundred and fifty-five square feet of it. My name is on my mailbox. I have two cotton futons rolled up in a corner awaiting sleep-filled nights when the sun goes down around five p.m. There's no gas yet so there's no hot water, so certainly no tea. I proudly mop like mad to get rid of carpenter's dust and the Toto toilet "newish" smell. I enjoyed a cold spit bath to refresh myself. My clothes hang on a closet rod that I must kneel to access. For total lack of storage, I will pile everything on shelves in this clever hideaway under the stairs and continue to live out of my suitcases.

September 1, 1989. I have come a long way in eight calendar days. I went out for pork noodles and beer with Shizuko last night. Very alive and noisy little town, brighter almost at night by neon than by day. Found futon and floor awfully hard, noise and fumes from traffic below difficult. Tomorrow is gas, refrigerator, and hot bath day!

So this is Gottano...but where are the children?

~

a
high regard of
the past
is the soul
of Japan

Wasurerarenai Kodomotachi

The Children, I Can't Forget the Children

Enrolled were names and faces of my girl pupils,
indelibly etched into my heart
and back of my eyelids for eternity

Three days later, Shizuko found the time to show me the ground floor school, soon to be Gotanno's first and only "School of English", the *Eigo Gakuin.* My request to her to do this was through a great deal of gestures, for besides our daily greeting, I had not a single word in common with my venerable landlady and new-found friend.

A tug on her arm brought the necessary key out of her pocket and with some resignation and embarrassment, she led me down a long, narrow and very dark tunnel to what was once her prestigious piano bar and nightclub.

What met my eyes and nose was ghastly! In eerie darkness, I stared into one big room, devoid of shape and any semblance to this once very successful gathering place. The thin walls had been stripped, taken down to bare, packed brick. The smell from damp wallpaper hanging in shreds was overpowering, and in the middle of the room, my eyes barely discerned the ashen pile and dry fronds from the Shinto priest's recent blessing of this site. Even in a remodel, custom has it that all old and evil spirits must be driven out completely, in order for the new establishment to thrive.

The space had been gutted in true Japanese fashion. I was looking at the steel girder skeleton of the Kato Building, designed to hold up the second and third floor and to sway in the earthquakes.

The tiny bathroom and fixtures remained, but had become a gathering place for a small colony of sizeable cockroaches. I marveled at their enormous size, their honey-gold shells, and how swiftly they moved. This was not the time nor place to be a squeamish schoolmistress, I thought!

Through Shizuko's sounds and gestures I gathered that she too was more than sorry at the state of things, and the Lowerys had voiced being heartily sorry things had not progressed very rapidly since the priest's ceremony. They blamed most of it on the building contractor, of course, "...but believe us, now that we have our teacher, things will move with incredible speed."

And they did. By the end of that week, twenty-four-hour-a-day crews had arrived and in quick succession forms were laid, cement poured and polished, walls went up, tile went down, windows and doors, and blackboards and white boards, and sound systems, and air conditioners were all installed. The desks and chairs and texts arrived, and in less than three weeks, we christened the tiny bathroom in blacks and greens, and mirrors with fresh flowers, and fans, and roach traps. We were going to have a school after all.

Then the sign was unveiled: "The J. G. Lowery School of English, Pahto Tulneh, *sensai*." Flyers went out, and an open house was held. In a demo class to prospective parents, I showed off the entire set of Cambridge and Oxford dictionaries, textbooks, and all but tap-danced on the desk tops with my Sesame Street Big Bird puppets—backed up by sing-along tapes presented on a Sony 35-inch TV screen with a high fidelity sound system.

As a result, by late October, I had one hundred and twenty-six native Japanese students, ages four to seventy-four, in a rigorous schedule that started at 2:00 p.m. promptly and ran to 10:00 p.m. Tuesdays through Fridays and all day Saturdays. I had Sundays and Mondays off for good behavior, or fatigue, whichever came first. And since I was working forty-two-hour weeks plus prep time, fatigue always won.

Enrolled were names and faces of my girl pupils, indelibly etched into my heart and back of my eyelids for eternity: Natsuko, Michiko, Junko, Etsuko, Tsuneko, Keiko—names usually falling into common constructions of Japanese characters or Chinese ideograms connoting such traits as fortitude, grace, colors, and beauty—and the bright and serious boy students: Akira, Akitoshi, Isao, Tohru, Yoshi, Yoshihiro.

Saturday's youngest children were my heart's delight because they were so fresh and eager and quickly overcame their inhibitions. Echoing commands and parroting were their forte. Short of a few gales of giggles, classes went like military clockwork. I did lots of visuals, flash cards, and hands-on, and the children learned quickly. By spring, their comprehension level was excellent and we were able to play many simple English circle and singing games with gusto. The "Hokey Pokey" was a lasting favorite.

The "tea party" classes I gave mid-day to mostly housewives bored with soap operas and overheated apartments were somewhat demoralizing and less challenging, because I felt they gathered in groups of eight to ten, (a) only to be able to tell their friends that in lieu of mid-life crises they were studying a foreign language, and (b) that it was a status symbol to have hired a foreigner to teach them a language, and certainly (c) it was wonderful to get out of their tiny little 2LDKs, (two-bedroom, living-room/dining room, kitchen) apartments—the approximate double-garage-sized homes they were captive to most of their married life. They only wanted to drink tea, giggle, and party, and seldom paid attention to the lessons or homework I assigned.

The ladies always brought elaborate pastries and looked forward to breaking from their "studies" early, eating and laughing, and staying on long into my dinner break. My discomfort at being a part of a highly verbal tea party then, being stared at, and most assuredly talked about, right in front of me, came to an end in the spring when I grew wise and was able to say, "*Eto, Eigo onegeishimasu*," meaning "Speak only in English please." That broke up the party fast!

Above all, and over the year's time, my pride and joy were my evening "juppie classes," those young Japanese professionals whose companies paid them to take English. Beginners though they were, these late evening students were highly motivated and they concentrated to a level of exhaustion at our two-hour sittings, struggling with the written, oral, and comprehensive level of English.

Because they were white-collar workers, both men and women with diverse backgrounds, we soon began to enjoy an intimacy brought to class by their intense curiosity about my country. They would bring up current events, news stories, politics, global issues, high profile personalities, and I began to see what a brazen and often harsh, loud, and often contemptible image we Americans have around the world.

The Japanese do see us through the distortions of Hollywood and videos to such a degree that it was personally demoralizing. Questions came up like: "Do all Americans use that kind of language? Carry guns? Shoot their mothers-in-law? Live in stucco mansions on the cliffs of Malibu?"

Here I was, with the monumental job of portraying to one small segment of the Japanese population the image of myself as an ordinary middle-class, struggling, widowed school teacher so fascinated with their amazing country and culture that I would strike out on my own to immerse myself in downtown Gotanno.

And they openly invited me to share with them my opinions and ideas, my values, and some of my triumphs and sorrows. They were curious about my Christianity and beliefs because they somehow struggle with their multi-theism; several had friends or relatives who had become Christians, and certainly those also living on Koudou Street had seen me truck off early every Sabbath for choir practice.

When I returned after Christmas holiday, I brought back photos of my family and friends, my Oregon rental home, my one-room schoolhouse in Brothers, (which was quickly likened to Pah-to's "Little House on The Prairie," seen daily at 5:30 in the afternoon on Japanese Public Television, with a rating comparable to "L.A. Law" or better), and they began to realize how overrated and glitzy their notions had been.

Far more fascinating to them was the fact that I, a big-boned, brunette Norwegian, and big John Paul, a sandy-haired, six-foot-six German, could give birth to three red-headed offspring, and go on to have blond, blue-eyed grandchildren and brunette, brown-eyed grandchildren! The gene pool discussion could have taken up countless hours.

I was grateful for my Norwegian weakness of talking with my hands, for between my comfort with acting out with Charades, and my fairly artistic talent of illustrating and cartooning on my eight-foot whiteboard, I could get just about any point across I needed or wanted to.

I was forever going to the board and reinforcing a lesson, and my successes were met with either stunning rounds of applause, gales of laughter, or weak, pinkish blushes and a degree of prudish embarrassment. I minced no words. I was, after all, already their beloved *sensai.*

With the title, position, pay, and workload came a certain level of prestige. Word had spread like wildfire in the town—who I was and where I lived and what I was there for. I had touched the neighborhood, for among my one hundred and twenty-six enrollees, I was teaching someone's grandson, a neighbor's grandson, or a neighbor's neighbor's grandson. I taught the liquor store owner's college-aged offspring, the florist's daughter, the dress-shop manager and her clerk, her son, and the druggist's mother…and I was treated in the local eateries and establishments quite well, a sort of silent respect I had yet to earn but was afforded me. My presence at their train platform began to elicit more polite greetings from strangers than stares at my oddity as the only foreigner there. I cherished that in my humble heart.

Some days word spread, apparently by phone. I would disembark from the train, buy a newspaper, wave my umbrella to the *soba* noodle shop lady, turn the corner past the fish house, *sushi* take-out bar, Pachinko gambling parlor, dry cleaners, *sembai* cracker bakery, to the dress shop on my block only to find my neighbors standing out on the sidewalk to greet me, "Hallo. Howar yew? Have a gooood day today?"

As fast as I walk, how, I wondered, did they know I was coming "home?"

But I was home. Gotanno was home.

One night, to my horror, I nearly cut off my right index finger on a broken wine glass in soapy dishwater. Without even thinking, I wrapped it up in a towel, and went running up the street two blocks in my nightie and robe to the pharmacy. No one thought a thing about this except to rescue their local *geijin*. The saintly druggist, young Mr. Ota, whom I shall never forget, and his wonderful, young, very pregnant wife, helped me through the faint and recovery stage, stopped the bleeding, stitched my finger from its severed and dangling position, wrapped it tightly and then sprinkled it generously with a nasty, green, fine powder of Chinese origin, I am sure.

For many days afterwards, Mr. Ota regularly changed the dressing at no cost. Today I see only a faint scar on my finger and remember their kindness.

Months after the finger incident, I took a favorite obsession of mine, a Snickers bar, out of my little black refrigerator freezer, bit down, and watched my upper right eye-tooth go zinging across the hardwood floor! Stunned at this sudden separation, and the shocking, gaping hole left in my smile in the mirror, I put it in my pocket and went trudging up the avenue to the local dentist, oddly enough on the second floor of my life-saving pharmacist's building.

He, with his lecherous grin, pocket dictionary, and rudimentary sign language, promptly glued it in with Japan's high-tech super glue, again at no cost to the patient. I had a most distressing whistley-lisp for the next three months until I could get home for summer furlough and have it remedied.

When I left Japan almost three years later, I took the train back out to Gottano just to say a special goodbye to Mr. Ota to explain to him I was leaving forever. Their healthy boy child was tucked in his mother's arms behind a shy smile and tears.

I felt a deep and personal sadness leaving all these people. They had opened their hearts and homes to me in downtown Gotanno.

These, then, were the first of my "Anna's children." I can never forget them, for they made me love my adopted children as much as my own.

O Joshiki, Ikisugi

Common Sense: Overload!

...heading off what I surmised to be south turned out to be west. I turned left and east, which turned out to be south!

In these first three months I found life in a foreign country not only a sensory overload where I reached my pillow in an exhausted state each and every night, but an experience where I needed to use every single ounce of common sense. My father, my inspiration and hero, gone now nearly five years, had always said, "Men have horse sense, women have common sense."

I prayed I had inherited both. Looking back now, were I to author another book, it would be titled, *The Complete Handbook of Geijin Mistakes: A Thorough, Graceful Way of Stumbling Through Japan.*

Seven days into my new life, in my fine, spanking-new apartment in this land of Sony, *samurai, sushi,* and *sake,* the laundry is mounting up. It is the first week of September and the "dog days" are upon us. If "perspire" is the politically correct things ladies do, then I sure as hell was sweating. Here, a person really cannot wear the same clothes two days in a row: salt lines begin to march where ring-around-the-collar once trod.

So I took myself down to Roppongi, a great shopper's paradise, on the Hibya Line subway. I came up under the giant Panasonic video screen, staring at the orange and blue spike hairdos on the black leather-vested young folk, and struck off to the famed Toyota showroom corner with the nearby row of street vendors, a particularly fascinating open-air shop with terrific Chinese imported goods.

There I fell in love with a three-gallon wicker basket that was tall enough, I surmised, to hold at least four days worth of laundry. With my upcoming teaching schedule, I would be lucky to get to the laundromat on my Sunday evenings, Mondays off, or some weekday, early before classes begin. It seemed four days worth should do it; anything larger than this basket would definitely not fare well on the rush hour trains.

I was ecstatic as I headed home with my basket and a bag of wooden clothespins. I was beginning to nest, Japanese style. I felt a powerful urge to do a load of wash!

Powder detergents, bleaches, softeners and every product available from the Proctor-Gamble galaxy right down through successful Amway monopolies may be found in this land of the sudsing and squeaky clean. But where are the laundries?

With the inner confidence of "Lassie Come Home," I put my new basket brimming with salty knickers and moldy towels under my right arm and set out with my newly-purchased neon orange box of what I clearly hoped was clothes soap and not some toilet scour product. I trod past my favorite supermarket. The electric-eye door opened and shut at my passing, disgorging what I believed was enough air conditioning to keep my tiny *apato* going for five hours. While I longed for AC, I acclimated to a great degree, mostly by hanging out down in the new classroom.

At the Emergency Clinic I asked the receptionist, bowing lowly, intonations of asking the polite question: *Shitsurei desu ka, Laundry-mat-o?* (Roughly translated: Excuse me, where's Laundromat?), throwing in my own gender ending, as if to be super polite. It seemed like a fair question. I've only been here a week.

No response, only a strange look. I crossed the *dori* (avenue) to the tiny pot-licker restaurant, and asked the same question again, only this time, chin up, with an adopted air of confidence. (If my father could only see me now, I am thinking already.)

Once more, I got a quizzical stare, no verbal response. I was tiring of the basket now, having switched arms twice, and the hundred-yen coins in my pocket were getting heavy. But I approached two pleasant ladies on my way back to the apartment who mutually shook their head, smiled oh-so-politely and muttered, *Wakanai* (I don't know).

Suddenly I understood what I believed to be the brightest power surge I've had so far in Nippon-land, the first one here—and probably the most important.

From this day on, for one score and eight months thereafter, I began to shift from knee-jerk reactionary acts to clear and crisp acts of common sense—common sense of survival caliber, to be exact.

I simply went back up to my apartment, got a small pad of paper and a pencil. I drew a clothesline from left to right, several garments of clothing, shoulders clearly punctuated with clever little vertical clothespins, even put a slight sway in the line as if it was a really big load. I marched right back to the Emergency Clinic desk, where the receptionist visibly winced when she saw me coming again. I showed her the picture without uttering a syllable.

She looked.

She brightened.

She popped out of her cubbyhole, stepped to the door and said, "Ah so, coin-oh-laundo-reee...," pointing not three hundred yards down a side alley off the supermarket parking lot. And there was a neon sign in blue on white, "Laundry-Maytag." I felt so at home.

Laundry-Maytag became my favorite haunt on Sunday nights at sundown, and usually late Monday dinner hours, for while my new friends, the Japanese of Gotanno, were slaving away over their two-burner gas flames and rice cookers, I was eating out at the pot-lickers' stand-up cafe while my laundry was washed and folded in my lovely new basket.

Being lost, can be frightening at any age. I have experienced it, to my memory, only once in the woods of southern Oregon, fortunately on a moonlit night when I tried to retrace my way to my U.S. Forest Service mountain lookout station.

Being lost in Tokyo is quite another matter, possibly devastating—and a postal, or *ku*-district, map will bear me out about this—there is neither rhyme nor reason to its grid. There are no two parallel slabs of asphalt road within a mile of each other.

So getting lost in Tokyo can be fairly disarming, in fact, unless, of course, you have inherited some place deep within yourself my father's keen common sense. Soon I was to feel him with me on this, my maiden journey.

After a couple of weeks busying myself in the new apartment, satisfied that everything was in its place—the school construction was moving right along, and I was feeling very comfortable yet restless with my long afternoons of freedom—I became curious about Gotanno proper and my neighborhood surroundings.

With nothing more than my fanny pack, house key, and some coins for an iced coffee, I strolled off mid-afternoon for what I thought would be an hour, at the most, of exercise. I admit that I have a fierce, egotistical sense of pride about possessing a compass in my head, where, at home in Oregon, the sun rises in the east over the mountains and sets in the west over the Pacific. In Japan, however, the sun rises in the east over the Pacific and sets in the west over Fuji and the mountains. I was in trouble.

Heading off what I surmised to be south turned out to be west. So I turned left and east, which turned out to be south. And while wandering down a fairly narrow and meandering, well-manicured residential street with block after block of fine, rose-covered, three-story apartment complexes, a rather loud internal alarm was going off inside me saying, "This isn't going quite right; you're leaning to the left too much, I mean north too far, I mean...you don't have any idea where in the world you are!"

And suddenly, I found myself in a great apartment complex playground, outfitted with every imaginable apparatus pre-schoolers could hope to have, yet devoid of children and laughter.

I stopped dead in my tracks.

My "I'm enjoying this plodding, relaxed walk" experience turned to stone. I saw not a living soul; not an open window, not one hungry, whining cat, nor rolling cycle, nor postman, friendly or otherwise. Turning a complete three hundred sixty degrees, I could not recognize the alleyway from which I had come to be here.

The walls of the apartments began to close in on me. The sun went behind a cloud. I found out later, it was Tuesday, the day the forty-two *ku* (counties) in Tokyo cremate, and the cloud was indeed slight ashfall and necessary smoke. I imagined for a moment my ears were plugged and I was involuntarily deaf. And the claustrophobia to which I am prone set in with a mild hysteria that produced a subcutaneous rash. My skin was alive and crawling!

My God! I was lost; I had absolutely no idea how to get out! Any one of the five alleys could take me deeper into the labyrinth from where I came, all in the wrong direction.

Weak with fear, I slunk down to sit on a curb in my new mantle of fatigue, heard a sound, and felt a surge of common sense overtake my inner being. Faint as it was, the train, on its elevated tracks, could be heard coming out of the east, which I thought was north, and I heard my father's voice clearly yet softly: *"Well done, Patti; you live one lousy block from the station. Get up and go home. Go to the station, then follow the train tracks back home."* His voice was so calm and reassuring.

I got up and broke into an almost flat-out run, winding first this way and that, but ever east, out of the Wonderland maze into which I had taken myself.

A welcome commuter train passes Gotanno's platform regularly every four minutes this time of the day, and increases to every two and a half minutes as the working populous belches out of their offices and homes to waiting bistros, wives, and families. As the train track clatter became louder, I slowed down as my fatigue diminished to just nervous frustration, and I allowed myself that welcomed iced coffee from one of dozens of vending machines stacked up along sidewalks nearly everywhere.

I could now smell the station.

At last, I rounded one more corner toward sunset and found myself under the tracks which I could now parallel to the station, and get more quickly home. I had been gone nearly ninety minutes.

After that, I never left home without a pad and pencil, carefully tracing the corners I turned so I could methodically work my way back again.

To this day I never read excerpts from "Alice" without choking up a bit, feeling that anxious sensation of a maze...and from then on, I usually stuck to well-traveled, taxi-laden *dori*'s.

Tracks and trains and my sense of hearing were keen allies in my survival. "Japan would never get the better of me," saith I.

Iwamoto-Ke: Subarashi Hitotachi!

The Iwamotos—My Wonderful Friends

Wine, sake, and song, swaying arm-in-arm,
and falling often into drunkenness and hilarity
can be the second language when stilted English fails.

On my third day in Gotanno, the Iwamotos became an important part of my life.

Three doors down from my new mailbox was the custom jeans and apparel shop, simply called "Maya," owned by Tsuneko Iwamoto, and her husband, Akira.

Tsuneko welcomed me to the community, came to the language school at two o'clock three times a week, and was leader of the tea party ladies. Tsuneko became a special friend in a way that almost belies words. She was a self-appointed Chamber of Commerce for Adachi-ku and is my Japanese "sister" to this very day. Her only child and son, Akitoshi, then twenty-seven, was a cultural exchange teacher in the

Dallas-Ft. Worth school district during the fall I arrived in Gottano. Since Tsuneko's shop was only three doors from my mailbox and front door, she was a first-day enrollee of the J. L. English School.

Tsuneko would see to it personally that my time spent in Gottano was a positive experience, matched only by the fine time her son was having in Texas and the big ten-gallon welcome mat the Texans had thrown out for him there.

To further this cause, Tsuneko enlisted many nearby shop owners to enroll in day classes and their teenagers to become part of an elite evening class for young adults, which I so enjoyed.

This dear friend desperately wanted to be able to converse with her son's host family, enjoy later travels to America, and befriend me. I was a status symbol. Her sixty-seven-year-old husband of thirty-one years, Akira, had been to Texas to visit his son, which meant he'd seen more of America outside Oregon than I ever had.

Akira owned a multi-million dollar, fine women's apparel manufacturing plant in Tokyo, and quickly became part of Tsuneko's mission, perhaps involuntarily, when *mama-san* said, a few days after the New Year, "It's Pat-oh's birthday, and we will throw her a party; please make us a guest list!"

That's when all Akira's factory workers came into my life—wonderful, warm friends like Keiko, Junko, Yoshihiro, and Toshiko. The event of a genuine Japanese birthday party is not to be missed in this life, so turning forty-eight in a foreign land with friends like these was a privilege.

Their very large, customized tea room held a plethora of individual bouquets, bottles of sake, and ribboned balloons, as these warm and wonderful strangers, bearing gifts, successfully replicated a good old American birthday party for me as I struggled to hold back a fierce case of homesickness and tears. Inside these bambooed walls they sang, *"Otanjobi! Pah-to"*—"Happy Birthday, Pah-to!" It was a birthday I shall never forget.

Wine, sake, and song, swaying arm-in-arm, and falling often into drunkenness and hilarity can be the second language when stilted English fails. By evening's end, I came to truly love all who had come that night to make me feel so welcome.

And it would be these dear people who would come together again three years later to surround me with heartfelt *sayonaras*.

After I returned to Oregon, folks back home often asked me whether Tsuneko and Akira's fine, long marriage was an arranged one or one for love. I believe with the Iwamotos' age difference, it could well have been arranged back in the late 1950s, Japanese matchmaker-style, when Tsuneko was but twenty-two and Akira was fresh out of the service, handsome and debonair at thirty-four years old. Yet never in my three years with them did I see two people more devoted to each other than the Iwamotos. They just sparkled together! And Kari, my youngest, and I would join them in Tokyo years later for their exclusive, fiftieth anniversary. Such is our friendship.

While Tsuneko is the typical "jump-up-when-father-wants-something" wife, he returns her deeds of kindness with untold spirit and gratitude. Their respect for each other, overt affection, warmth, giggles, and just plain delight in each other's company was always so refreshing in a country where spousal "preoccupations"—the custom of having a mistress—abounds.

It took me three years to observe first-hand and appreciate, after many road trips with Akira, how low-profile and exceedingly humble he is. As the owner/operator/entrepreneur in the ladies fine apparel industry, operating a large factory on the eastern outskirts of the city, he was indeed, one of the leading fabricators in all of Tokyo. He maintained a finely-tuned home-industry network of seamstresses, all of whom I met when I had the privilege of accompanying Akira on extended road trips. I thought it was a grand way to see the country on my days off; he enjoyed the company I believe, though our communication was confined to hand talk and lunch out.

Akira would deliver huge bandana-wrapped bundles called *firoshikis,* parcels of pre-cut fabric, so that invalid or house-bound elderly women might assemble his garments piece-meal and thus be self-supporting. I found this aspect of his business very heart-warming and an important key to the success of his operation.

His fashions sold only in the million dollar real-estate shops around the city. Some were exported to selected sites and cities in southern and western Honshu. Tsuneko also featured his garments at Maya, of course.

The emotional and sincere investment he had in each of his employees was apparent with each delivery—all hugs and gusto greetings. And when he and I walked into the factory unannounced, everything halted and everyone bowed deeply and reverently…he just smiled widely and waved them back to work.

The devotion to employer by employee is second only to the family, for Japanese companies have a system of lifetime employment; retirement age is sixty in Japan. Akira's employees were no exception. He was the master of the workforce and enjoyed employee allegiance, yet he always socialized with them on many, many occasions. For Akira, all one hundred fourteen factory workers: managers, sub-managers, designers, cutters, stitchers, assemblers, piece-mealers, salespersons, and store managers, from Nagoya to Nigata to Kyoto, were simply family.

The following year, on the occasion of my monumental forty-ninth birthday, Akira, in the tea room of his mansion in Chiba, lifted his *sake* glass to toast me and welcome me, saying in halting English "Be, from this day, as my wife: beloved and always welcome." I knew I had been accepted like few other foreigners are, into a culture I could respect, revere, and humble myself. From that day on he never called me *Pat-san* (Missus Pat) again, but rather *Pat-o-chan,* a suffix of endearment.

The sense of family is fiercely defined, defended and protected by all Japanese. And to Akira Iwamoto I was now *Pat*-o-*chan*.

During my second year in Japan, after a trek to Oregon for summer school coursework in Colorado for autistic children, I held a five-day-a-week teaching job in a very special school. I longed to keep in touch with the Iwamotos and suddenly I had my weekends free to spend time in their garden and the peace it afforded me.

Tsuneko arranged that I would come then for bimonthly "homestays," as she fondly called it. This allowed me an amazing view to the lifestyle, religious rituals, and the honor and strict regimen of a Japanese family with one child. Their son, Akitoshi had returned from Dallas and we had quickly become quite good friends over Hollywood movies and some karaoke washed down with *sake*. Very soon, the doors swung open for our relationship as "family."

It was a half-hour train ride and several transfers above ground for me, from old Gotanno to Chiba prefecture, but I quite enjoyed the less crowded cars and the scenery out east to Kashiwa City and to the Iwamotos' Chiba mansion. More often than not, I left late Friday after work, slept in the mansion, then drove with Tsuneko and Akira to this "new school," for Akira had, wishing to be a part of the growing trend toward "English school," solicited over a dozen long-time friends of the Iwamoto family to become patrons of *his very own* language school in Kashiwa City, population well over a million. He therefore rented a large, handsome modular which sat at the edge of a big shopper's parking lot, just minutes from the train station. And he had hired me to be his *sensai.*

There, on Saturday, twice a month, I would travel out for a "homestay" and I held court at the fine white boards from eight to ten o'clock—not counting tea and cakes and "happy hour" with these lovely ladies in a very formal, very beginning English school.

Fitting into his hectic schedule, Akira would be the sole male student on these very, very early Saturday mornings. I felt he quite liked being with his Saturday "harem" of giggling lovely ladies—some of them lifelong, childhood friends of this sixty-seven-year-old patriarch. So many of them came from his homeland in Wakayama-ken in southern Honshu, near Osaka, and had since migrated to the callings of Tokyo fortunes with families and spouses. In class, Akira's military stature overwhelmed the room, if you can picture that, and he sported the finest of suits and ties, his shiny, pomade-hair reflecting the offensive and always over-done use of fluorescent lights.

For the next two years, commuting from first Naka-Meguro and later Musashi-Sakai, where I enjoyed new jobs and salary raises each spring, I would continue in this little trailer school by the parking lot, and witness the emotional reunions with new adult students at the Kashiwa school. Akira had so many fast friends. I continued to be under his tutelage as *sensai.* This was the Iwamotos' way of keeping contact with me, my way of bonding with them, and the way I came to see the width and breadth of Japan, by being part of this great and generous family. And with the growing friendship with their son Akitoshi, I had a new, little Japanese brother to translate for me, while I fine tuned his English—our own "classes" often being held over *sake*!

The Iwamotos' closest friends were three very handsome and devoted couples, always present at New Year's celebrations, often on birthdays and other high festival days, friends who knew each other from their high school years together back in Wakayama, in southern Honshu, and who remained fast friends in the five decades since.

Akira loved throwing parties in his great tea room. The wives attended our school; the husbands showed up for the parties. Coming from an American, upwardly mobile society where even siblings rarely gathered, except for funerals and lesser occasions, I was quite moved to witness the deep affection among these couples. And here in bustling Tokyo, the Iwamotos had managed to maintain childhood bonds despite the hundreds of miles separating these persons from the homeland of their clans.

The Iwamoto mansion is two miles from Kashiwa City station in a most pleasant, quiet suburb full of magnificent gardens, orange trees, poinsettia bushes big as garages, magnolias, azaleas, and lovely two-story homes of residential nature. Within walking distances are the amenities of a main bus line, a Domino's Pizza, numerous eateries, a bakery, barber shops, a market, and small parks for dog walking.

There is no day of rest *per se* for either students, parents, or the community. Education and fitness are a national, cultural standard to which all seem to comply. During my stays there, I woke regularly early Saturdays to the echoes of fireworks and public address-system announcements proclaiming the day's sports and fitness events soon to take place at the nearby high school field, usually at five in the morning!

Tsuneko was utterly dismayed when I told her I loved to "sleep in" on Saturday. "You very selfish person! Need to rise early and make the most of each day!" she'd cry. To which I replied, "No thank you. I like being selfish unto myself."

Set high on a steep, retaining wall, the Iwamotos' modern, two-story home towers over the duplexes below. Ten years ago, on the site of their honeymoon home, the old house was traditionally leveled to the ground, swept clean by bamboo brooms, and blessed by a Shinto priest. Akira and Tsuneko speak of the six months living over their jeans shop out of boxes as this new home was erected by a leading contractor.

So successful was their magnificent home that it was featured in a television ad for a very intimate tour of the home, given by Akira and Tsuneko in their traditional dress kimonos and *hakamas* (female and male traditional dress). Modern by every American standard, yet Japanese to the ultimate detail, their mansion is a breath-taking blend of finest of woods, *tatami* mat, bamboo, *shoji* screen partitions, thermal panes, and sliding patio doors. All this, leading to the intensely manicured garden where I sought hours of solace throughout the four seasons over my three years there.

And it's there my mind and heart, even now, frequently wander...

My first morning in that garden, Tsuneko had slipped down the hardwood hallway in her brisk, familiar shuffle, slid open the *shoji* of the tea room where I lay, and whispered "*Pah-to-san,* wake, please!—beee-u-tiful day. Come sit in the sun."

Having first arrived very late the night before, I quickly put on my navy cotton *yukata* (bathrobe), slipped into my "zori" sandals, and accepted the steaming mug of hot coffee she had so graciously brewed for me.

I had no idea what awaited me.

There before me were stone steps, edged in lush green grass that was *not* to be stepped upon. Rather, carefully placed stones showed where one could walk in The Garden.

An area perhaps twelve feet square was edged and hedged with magnificent shrubbery, azaleas, boxwoods. A monolithic, solitary, smooth boulder resembling an Elizabeth Taylor pendant stood sentinel in the far west corner, some five feet high and thousands of years old. Carefully shaped *bonsai* maples, now green with spring and new life, leaned into the garden as if to bow and welcome me. Over the stone waterfall stood a marvelous flowering *ume* (plum) tree, from which they would harvest the fall fruits for a traditional homemade batch of *ume-bochi* (pickled plum preserves), another eat-for-good-fortune food brought out on special occasions only.

There, to my surprise and delight, was a magnificent, virgin-white gardenia bush, loaded with flowers that made the late dawn air pungent, causing an untimely pang of homesickness in the pit of my stomach as this was my parents' and my own wedding flower.

Tsuneko slipped away, as quietly as she had come, perhaps to allow me the quiet time for worship solitude that goes with The Garden, and, no doubt, from seeing the tears that glistened in my eyes as I was swept away by the beauty and solitude of this wonderful place.

Birds came and went, darted and flirted with my thoughts. The sun made its way over my shoulder and onto my robe, warming my head and heart, as yet another wave of "where am I anyway?" sensations washed over me.

I am really, really here, in Japan—wrapped in its history, beauty and splendor! Triumph coupled with overwhelming humility pounded in my breast. The Iwamotos would make it all happen.

Then I heard something faint yet unrecognizable, and leaned toward the smooth marble Buddha basin. I saw the slow trickle of water come down the split bamboo pipe, drop into the basin, then overflow and fall off the sides. It trickled into the shallow pond below, and disappeared into a carved-out shaft, dark in the shadows. There, within the basin—and typical of garden respites and traditional Japanese waterfalls of man-made nature—lay two brass bells, corded to tinkle when the water strikes them.

It was muted magic to my ears. So subtle—suggesting, perhaps, that the senses of a person have to be romanced, but the heart and mind must be quiet in its presence in order to receive the outpouring.

I hold this all, in my heart, forever.

Chonan, Hitorikko

First and Only One, Akitoshi

My beloved little Japanese "brother," Akitoshi, moved home from Dallas in the summer of 1990 and quickly became (and continued to be) the point card in my deck as far as bridging the sometimes frustrating language barrier with his parents, my host family.

This very personable and special "Number One Son" and only child of my host family, Aki was born on January 4, and therefore *beloved gift* to this family in the New Years week. In Japan, a child born in the first seven days of a New Year is "very special."

Unmarried and in his early thirties, it was a particular delight for me to gain the little brother I'd never had—someone to hassle, tease, and he to be there to translate my way out of frequent "pickles and dilemmas."

I began to get to know Aki in my first year of friendship with his mother via the wonderful telephone satellite from Texas. He was hosted that year by the Brownlee family in Grand Prairie, Texas, an affluent Dallas suburb, where he was a cultural exchange teacher in the Dallas-Ft. Worth junior high schools.

Going from school to school in that district, Aki taught everything from Japanese beginning language and origami to history and culture, his winning smile and extrovert personality bringing everything alive.

It delights me now when, despite sixteen clock hours difference, he telephones at odd hours with a "Hall-o, how-wahr-yo-u-u?" in his lilting, sing-song voice. We have shared the love of many baseball games, countless blockbuster DVDs, Sumo events, hearty meals, train rides, and excursion boat rides since.

But in the wee hours of my home-stays watching Hollywood movies, I have been challenged to explore his inquisitive mind and to help explain the many cultural innuendos presented in those movies that Aki recognizes but cannot quite place or sort out. Those times gave us a rare opportunity to share thoughts and opinions and mine the depths of our culture's manners and mores.

Over the next two years, in exchange for my bimonthly homestay experiences in Kashiwa with his parents, Aki received many extemporaneous English lessons that I was privileged to give to all three Iwamotos. We would gather in the family dining room around, or "under," the great cedar *kotatsu*—the low table with a built-in, infrared heating unit underneath, designed to be covered with a floor-length cloth to contain the heat and warm us—eating or drinking, always laughing and doing some sort of hand gesturing to finish the unfinished sentences.

I can still smell the vast *tatami* mats and incense on the family altar. I can still see the ten-foot pink azalea tree blooming out on the western patio. Over three years, I memorized every square foot of this traditional home, the warmth, the safety, and the decadent comfort I felt there.

Number One Son, while still at home, traditionally enjoyed the best of secondary education and a mother who still wakes him in the morning, feeds him, calls his taxi to the station, issues the appropriate train tickets, probably a lunch allowance, does his laundry, cooking, and kicks him out to the tennis courts to meet his peers on weekends, then shoveling out his bedroom in his absence—as tidiness is not one of his strengths.

Aki in turn is reverent and endearing with his mother; gentle teasing banter goes on constantly. He continually challenges his mother's faltering English. They are quite at ease with each other with public displays of fondness. He will forever be a devoted only child.

Like most young Japanese males with an indifference to the courtship scene, however, Aki was often pestered openly regarding matrimony or involvement with the traditional matchmaker. To my knowledge, his favorite Aunt Naoko in Osaka, mother's elder brother's lovely wife, served as his matchmaker. This would ensure the likelihood of a Wakayama miss becoming the next generation of Iwamotos' matron.

I asked my little brother once—in typical American/Hollywood fashion—"Aki, do you hope to marry for love or even a few ounces of infatuation?" His well-rehearsed reply was a blasé, "Oh no, certainly not! Just as long as she knows she has to live with my family, take care of my mother after father dies. She *must* be able to get along with my mother...love comes later."

"Ahhh so," I sighed...in resigned understanding.

A very clever young man who had a rich and positive American home-stay visit, Aki used the abundance of English films to keep on top of his pronunciation and comprehension. This second-language skill opened doors in industry for two decades, such that he now resides in Hong Kong in the import/export business of women's accessories.

It delights me that he took my advice that night, "Aki, marry for love!" And he is married to his Mandarin language teacher, lovely Kaori, whom he met and courted while assigned in Hong Kong with Motorola. Now they raise their own Number One Son, Shin, born serendipitously on grandfather Akira's May birthday.

Their family business affords him daily conversation with the American and Taiwan mainland, and frequent business trips throughout all of southeast Asia. He always calls me on my birthday and has been to Oregon twice now to play "cheap golf" and enjoy my family and home. My children adore him.

How lucky I am to have my favorite Number One Little Brother.

Jishin to Chichi No Ikari

Earthquake! And Fear of the Fathers...

Japanese fear three things, and in this order:
the wrath of their fathers, earthquakes, and fire.

On my forty-eighth day in Japan, my diary reads: *Saturday, Oct. 14. Woke at 0622 to my entire building swaying east to west, my futon sliding across the hardwood floors, and my head slamming into the wall; building was moaning and creaking. A quake of 5.9 on the Richter, I would later learn on F.E.N., Far East Network, the English-language military radio. Wow! Thought I was dreaming! Went back to sleep for two hours though. Hung out my bedding on the roof and had a lovely leisurely breakfast...*

Such nonchalance over earthquakes would not always be the norm, but my casual reference to my very first Nipponese *jishin* (earthquake), reflected once more my earnest desire to accept everything this country would offer up to me.

Japanese have a well-worn saying, "Japanese fear three things, and in this order: the wrath of their fathers, earthquakes, and fire."

I thought this was the most interesting commentary on their culture. Now it would seem earthquakes have eclipsed the wrath of fathers, because they were becoming more frequent, and the older generation was much more tolerant of the new generation and their wrath no longer held such weight.

In earlier days, largely because of the wood and paper construction of homes, gas fires, gas heaters, and gas stoves, major conflagrations followed strong earthquakes, as happened in nearby Kobe in 1995, three years after I returned home. Nonetheless, earthquakes, I would soon find, are most frequent in Japan and legend has it that a giant *"namazu"* (catfish) is wiggling its tail under the earth. Schools and places of work have frequent earthquake drills and I was very mindful of "gas off, windows open, duck, tuck, and roll under something like a table," a sequence they suggested in the drills.

The windows on my second floor were far too small for me to ever fit through, however, and with my claustrophobia, I found this very scary. My own *kotatsu* was about knee-high from the ground and would hardly have accommodated my tuck and roll, although it would have protected my neck and shoulders.

I wrote another earthquake diary entry four months later. It had been a particularly wet, cold, and snowy winter with temperatures hovering in the low thirties, and I was constantly shivering. This particular day, a Kyushu island "chinook wind" blew up from the south, rocketing temperatures to a rare and delightful sixty degrees—false spring, I thought. Warm and welcome winds, what a surprise. This was Sunday, February 11, 1990.

I made my way to church, choir practice, lunch with friends and, since I was scheduled for a homestay with the Iwamotos, I spent an afternoon of bumming through the super malls in Kashiwa City before arriving for one of Tsuneko's wonderful *sukiyaki* feasts and some equally welcome English-subtitled TV.

At the Iwamotos I was bathed and in bed by 10:30, reading myself to sleep with a fresh edition of *The Japan Times*. The next day, Monday, was a national holiday, Founder's Day, and I would get a chance to sleep in!

I was awakened at 2:46 a.m. to a strong jolt, a 5.5 on the Richter, centered on the Chiba Peninsula, and I was never able to go back to sleep after that. Even the Iwamotos' fine, modern home, recently built and the best of contemporary construction, clattered and rattled with this one—a "bouncer" as it was called. Much of the hillside where the Iwamotos' home is located was recent fill dirt, and it reacted to this sudden jolt, as did the seawalls at Kobe, where the newest of Japan's airport runways on the sea simply slipped away in the 1995 quake, reminding all of new construction methods and man's urgency to create "new land." Many of Japan's wide, white, east coast beaches are new land—white coral sands shipped up from Australia and blown onto reef territories just offshore to attract their urban populace to coastal resort towns.

Some earthquakes sink, some bounce, some rattle, some roll… all *jishins* are nerve-wracking and totally unannounced. It was when telephone poles swayed in their asphalt footings, and electric and telephone wires took up the cadence like jump ropes that I got a little frightened and braced inside the metal doorways whenever possible. Perhaps the wrath of a father would have been welcome relief to the frequent, irritable tremblings of the catfish's tail!

In the morning, Tsuneko burst into my shade-darkened room at 5:15 a.m., announcing we would soon be late for the "Early Morning Garden Club!"

"What?" I moaned; this was to be *my* day off! Without even so much as a bite to eat, we cabbed to a small trailer near the train station where some fifteen shy and giggling middle-aged friends of hers had gathered for an ultimately boring lecture on roses, the planting and pruning of the species, complete with flip charts and fine, watercolor illustrations. Given in Japanese, the lecture and presentation were not very enlightening for me.

I would realize later that I was taken along only to be shown as Tsuneko's new *geijin* friend. Hours later, over a scrumptious breakfast of curried chicken livers, omelette, miso soup, spinach and fresh fruit, Tsuneko would point to the dictionary and pound on the word *rikoteki,* a word for "selfish," meaning I am "too self-centered, choosing to sleep rather than rise before dawn and get the most out of life!"

Ahhh, the wrath of a mother...perhaps as much to be feared as the father?

More about the Kobe earthquake:

The Kobe earthquake, January 17, 1995, was a 7.2 Richter scale, near-surface quake, often referred to as The Great Hanshin because of the spectacular collapse of the Hanshin expressway, killing 6,434, injuring over 26,000, and causing to Japan an economic loss of nearly $US 200 billion.

Kyoto: Shizuka Na Ishidetami

Kyoto, Calm and Quiet Walking Stones

...muted by the early spring air, tinted in a magic blue haze,
and blessed by the wonderful plum and cherry blossoms
laying confetti pathways.

"This is insane," I kept telling myself, "absolutely insane." I had just worked five non-stop evenings at the English School and was moonlighting days teaching fifth grade at the prestigious American School in Japan (ASIJ) for another teacher on maternity leave.

Insane, yes, but spring had given me a restless energy that an additional teaching job satisfied, not to mention that I was fully enjoying the phenomena of being able to add extra money to my off-shore accounts.

No question that I was fatigued after those eighteen-hour work days, but on this particularly holiday weekend, being bone tired didn't stop me from queueing up at nearly midnight on Track Number 8 behind hundreds of very proper Japanese bound for mystical, magical, spiritual Kyoto. Once the ancient capital of Japan, the name Kyoto literally translates to "capital city" and remained so until 1603 when the Tokugawa, one of the feudal regimes of Japan, moved the seat of government to Edo, the Tokyo of today.

Kyoto is the center of Japanese culture and Buddhism. It was the only great city to escape bombing in WWII, thus preserving its ancient charm and treasures. My excitement experiencing my first spring in this "blossom kingdom of the world" could hardly be contained. To add to the adventure, no one in Gotanno knew of my leave-taking. One did not simply trek to Kyoto *hitoride*!

I hadn't a crystal-ball clue of what nine more hours, sitting straight up on a third-class train doing a milk run to the southern portion of greater Honshu, would do to my bones. I suspected that there would by a price to pay pushing my body in a twenty-nine-hour marathon—not to mention whatever sporadic sleep I might get.

I only knew that I simply had to celebrate spring and the plum blossoms and premature cherry blooms in Kyoto; it was so much the right and proper thing that my excitement overruled my common sense.

Shortly after midnight, the green- and cream-colored "midnight special" pulled into the station very slowly, and the human sea surged to get into their seats. I managed a window seat; by dawn I would be freezing and my fatigued body rheumatic.

I found myself knee-to-knee and toe-to-toe with a stunningly handsome, middle-aged father who sat his adolescent son next to me. He smiled a most pleasant greeting and gestured the offer to put my backpack up on the overhead rack, which I greatly appreciated and allowed him to do. I found most Japanese males extremely gallant and gracious to strangers. It goes with their fierce pride of the country, and wanting to make a good impression on foreigners, I am sure.

The train rolled out at exactly the appointed moment, and I watched the ports of Tokyo and Yokohama with their pulsating night lights dim on the seaward side of my train car.

By 1:30 a.m. I was fast asleep, already chilled to the bone under my bulky ski sweater, my shoulder bag serving as a pillow.

For the entire three hundred miles southward to the heart of Kyoto, this "local" train stopped at *each and every* red dot town on my map. In blurred succession and degrees of dawning, I saw dozens of sleepy-eyed folk tumble off in the mountainous foothill stations with their ski gear and backpacks to transfer perhaps to the resort towns of Guma-ken and Nigata.

I watched two-generations of families scurry off and be met on the platform by gaggles of squawking, long-lost relatives. The expense of travel, I knew, precluded frequent reunions, and time spent away at leisure was also a relative unknown to these dedicated working families, fleeing the metropolis for a precious and memorable spring weekend.

I did not have to be back to work until Tuesday at five in the afternoon because of my Sunday-Monday days off. Ecstasy! But even traveling third class, this trip was costing me a fair bundle. The Bullet Train was well over $300 round trip; the cost to ride this milk train was somewhere around $70, which I had saved for and planned on since Christmas.

Through the gracious Japan Tourist Bureau (JTB), housed downtown under the familiar logo of a giant red question mark, I had arranged for a spare, capsule-room near the Kyoto station at $70 per night so I would have a hot soak tub for my weary walking feet each night. Already visions of crisp white sheets were dancing in my head.

Dawn melted into daybreak in a thick mist of ground fog and dew, masking what I believed was a marked change in the landscape of southern Honshu. Traveling into the tea harvest prefectures, or counties, of the south, I rejoiced at seeing my first tea fields—tiny little manicured hedgerows of brilliant green, resembling round loaves of fresh bread lined up end to end. Japan now took on a semblance of wide valleys and broad base flood plains, much like the Napa Valley. Even the cast of the clay soil looked coppery, baked, and terra-cotta to me. This could account for the color of some of the potteries known from here, I told myself.

Then the number of rooftops multiplied in just minutes, a clue we were nearing the outskirts of bustling Kyoto.

We passed through a long impressive mountain tunnel to emerge on the Kyoto side of the Tamba-Kochi Mountains that surround Kyoto on three sides and right under Mt. Hie, elevation 2,810 feet. The Japanese, familiar with the station names, began the countdown with head and body language to spouse and children, and at each stop assembled their goods from the racks overhead, straightened their ties, and went through the motions of readying for rapid disembarkation.

Kyoto is a major railway terminal, and from high atop the Kyoto Tower, not unlike the Seattle Space Needle, one may see the high contrast of Shinkansen bullet trains as well as every reliable little local train as they pull proudly out of the station, north or south, one every three minutes of the day.

Later, I would meet two executives from the then-ailing Canadian National Railway, in the Kyoto Tower the next afternoon. Engrossed in the precision below, they were quick to tell me they'd been sent abroad to study the ever-awesome Japan National Railway System—the JNR, as it is fondly referred to—with its impeccable safety record.

It was a bit past nine o'clock Sunday morning now. It felt good to shake out and walk and gulp some fresh air in Kyoto this Sabbath morning. Ah, Patricia, "Sabbath" is not exactly the word one might use in the holiest of grounds to the Buddhist-Shinto capital of a Buddhist-Shinto nation, Kyoto. What do the Japanese call their holiest of holy days—if not a Sabbath? To me it was just a gorgeous Sunday!

I never thought to ask this of my Iwamotos, who were less than ritualistic openly, save visiting historic temples, shrines, and scenic destinations. Fact is, any day was a holy day when the Japanese wished to make it so. Akira takes an annual, personal pilgrimage every August during the "dog days" of summer. He visits eighty-eight Buddhist temples on the island of Shikoku, related to the priest Kobo-Daishi, over a period of four holiday days, ferrying there with his automobile so he may get around. And this he must do for ten years straight in order to attain his "holy perfection," as he called it, under the law of his elected religion, the Shingon-Mikkyo—or True Word—sect of Buddhism. It seems to me that the Shinto religion is very personally accommodating and their gods so compliant to the average "salaryman."

I checked in ever so briefly at my six-story "compact hotel," one cut above a youth hostel, but with a morning breakfast spread that would more than make up for the lack of amenities. I checked out the white sheets, the window view of another building scarcely seven inches away, the *ofuro* tub, and exchanged my trusty backpack in a dollar-coin locker for my fanny-pack, passport, cash, and travel book. Then I was off on a dead run to catch a bus for the foothills of Kyoto, not to waste a moment of daylight!

Like a good omen, or certainly a signal to put away my hot pink raincoat, the sun broke out. As the city bus lumbered noisily through the menacingly narrow streets, and huffed to the top of the hill turning around at the famed gold pavilion of Ginkgo Temple plaza, the day became increasingly warm.

Common sense and a little homework had told me that if I rode out to the far west outskirts of the city and followed the famed Philosopher's Walk, I would be sure to find most of the key tourist attractions, epitomes, and pulse of ancient Kyoto.

Standing in the ticket line at the Kinkakuji Temple, a fourteenth century masterpiece I had put at the top of my list, things moved swiftly and silently, a preface to the awe and whispering that would surround this emperor's ancient summer palace and landscaped grounds. I was pleased to be issued both a ticket and guide book in English from the very tourist-oriented National Treasure Pavilion headquarters.

I fell in behind a well-dressed young couple escorting their very elderly mother. Their body language told me they seemed anxious to make friendly conversation, as to welcome me to this most time-honored place, and of course practice their conversational English. I obliged them by suggesting, once we reached the bamboo rail beside the breathtaking mirror-like lake, they take my picture. This gesture was reciprocated on their Konica pocket camera, and we waved friendly waves each time we saw one another that morning. I cherish my picture of this delightful family to prove I stood at the shore of this magnificent reflective pond.

I have since tried to paint the intense blue-greens of the velvet hills arising from those morning salt-sea clouds, but some things in nature simply cannot be replicated. Still, I can shut my eyes and smell the crisp spring air, see those foothills, and hear the silence that fell upon the crowds.

Very soon our pathway and the traffic arrows sent visitors up a rather broad set of flat stone steps, some ninety yards, to man-made waterfalls that I could hear but not see. Glancing down so as not to lose my footing on steps still wet with dew in the dark forest glade,

I stopped dead in my tracks and dropped to my knees abruptly to explore what I thought my eyes perceived.

Instantly, the dozens behind me began to gasp, whisper, question, stoop, and stare also. My fingers traced deep images of ferns and leaves in these ancient flagstones that were fossilized, abundant with clear pictures of the world's past mastery. I was simply breathless at the discovery and could not communicate a thing. I did, however, recognize phrases from the natives akin to, "Look! Look what the *geijin* has discovered!"

Their faces told me they were so pleased that I, a poor, miserable, sinning Christian had taken delight in the magnificent choices made some two thousand years ago by their honorable stepping-stone artisans.

Now, will someone tell me, did the underpaid civil servants who daily take their handmade, crude twig brooms and clean away the day's soot and foot dust ever once notice or remark of this marvel to others? Were they not afraid that over the decades, thousands upon thousands of sandals, and Nikes, and Adidas would erode and erase this wonderful trace of prehistoric times?

Of course, I was not the first *geijin* to find the hidden mysteries of the golden temple's pond, but I'm humbled by having deep vision that day and the gift of enjoying the little things. And now I think I know why earth's poets who share the written word can tell of things they see that others never see. It made my voyage complete—almost another omen to my magical weekend getaway in treasure-laden Kyoto.

As I traveled aimlessly down the famed Philosopher's Walk, those ahead of me, dressed in spring pastels, were often elderly couples, arm-in-arm, or quietly giggling women in small tour groups. Today I was probably among the youngest persons enjoying the historic journey.

I savored the manicured grounds of the Shorenin Temple, Nanzenji Temple, and the awe-inspiring Manchurian red pagoda spire of Yasaka

Shrine. Goose bumps enveloped me as I took in the incredible cliff-side dwelling of the Buddhist Kiyomizu Temple's vast wooden porches. Overlooking a canyon choked with madrona trees and tropically twined underbrush, about as inviting as a lion's snare, I wondered how many unworthy servants or concubines might have met their demise in the ravine below?

Sunset became a silent, smoky, lingering twilight. Aware I had been afoot now for nearly nine hours, this foot-dragging tourist-about-town caught the late, very crowded bus back to the railway terminal where I would enjoy a wonderful *tempura* dinner plate, light beer, and some second-hand smoke in a rowdy taverna. As I made my way back to the capsule hotel with its starchy white sheets, visions of a long soak in my mini-tub hurried me along.

Kyoto had not disappointed me one moment of this perfect day.

This day was brushed with the early spring air, tinted with a magic blue haze, and blessed by the wonderful plum and cherry blossoms laying confetti pathways for the footsteps of the thousands of others who enjoyed this day with me.

~

Gardens so quiet you whisper.
Foot paths so ancient
built of fossiled stones.
Dedicated sweepers,
caretakers of history-
Faithfully gathering
winter's dry leaves.

Natsukashii Kamogawa

Somehow I Missed Kamogawa!

...mobs, literally mobs, of visitors, tunneling in from arteries all over Japan to the sacred home of the Great Daibutsu—Great Buddha.

Because there are no less than twelve national holidays in Japan and three major holiday times when most Japanese attempt to get out of town and to their homeland, (the assumption is half of Tokyo's eighteen million are not natives), holidays can be events to either avoid or be part of. Out of sheer ignorance, I preferred the latter, wanting to be a part of all national pasttimes

My diary reads: *"Holiday! Walked six hours at Kamakura, not by choice: bought the wrong ticket."*

On Tuesday, October 10, National Culture Day of my very first year in Tokyo, I woke to blue skies, having overslept a bit, but decided I yearned to be at the sea. I had to really haul to get to greater Tokyo station, and I confidently bought my ticket for Kamogawa, on the Boso Peninsula. Except that the ticket master heard "Kamakura," and motioned me down into the belly of the underground on a great escalator, Track Eleven. When we emerged into daylight, my radar knew we were headed southwest instead of east. And by 10:10, with amazingly light holiday traffic, I said to myself, "Wherever I'm going... oh, what the hell."

I arrived in Kamakura at 11:30 a.m. into mobs, literally mobs, of visitors, tunneling in from arteries all over Japan to the sacred home of the Great Daibutsu—Great Buddha—one of perhaps three most photographic landmarks in all of Japan—Mt. Fuji, and the floating *torii* gate Shrine at Miyajima Island being the other two.

For me the wonderful thing about melting into a festival crowd was that all I had to do was follow the natives, who read the signs and knew the way, to end up at some rewarding destination. I was game for anything under these gorgeous blue skies. By noon it was hot and I was wearing my jacket on my hips.

It turned out that Kamakura as a popular day-tripping town from Tokyo was completely user-friendly; many signposts were labeled in English, giving the names of the temples and shrines and the distance to the next key point of interest. Most points of interest had plaques at the gates explaining the history in English, and handsome brochures given out with the entry fees. I would go and enjoy the sights, then go home and later read about them, to implant the edifice in my mind.

Example: The Great Buddha! I had a very hard time imagining how large a temple must have been to house this forty-four-foot high Buddha, plus pedestal, then to picture the tidal wave of 1495 that swept away the temple, leaving this serene bronze statue out in the open for seven centuries since. A wave, leaping one mile inland from the sea that spawned such a storm, incredible!

Nature has not always been kind to the great archipelago of Japan with her tidal waves and Kanto Plain earthquakes. The dozens of monsoons and earthquakes I would experience in my three years were but a reflection of her angry power.

Kamakura is like the Sausalito of the Miura Peninsula, tastefully punctuated with eateries, coffee houses, souvenir shops, artistry shops, antique shops, and grand gardens and residential grounds. I liked to respectfully "snoop" into people's backyards and see how the citizenry lived. Aha! They too hang laundry out on sunny days, and use coffee cans for cigarette butts. Occasionally I would see a doghouse, but family pets were conspicuous by their absence, as were pet stores.

Cemeteries and monuments, even the grave of the wife of the great Black Ship pirate, Perry, could be found along a main street.

I began my collection of gentle brass wind chimes there and unique single pieces of eating pottery. I probably returned to Kamakura far more times than any one single day trip to share it with my many American guests over the years—Nancy, Zelia, Kari, Robyn—because of the cleanliness and serenity and lung-purging sea air. I came here many times to escape the madness of Tokyo and avoid madness itself.

With Kakamura's many fine small hotels and restaurants, I could wander up and down for hours and always end up back in at the looming alpine-like train station and bustling town square, a small, Picadill-ian Circle just jammed with local buses and mad taxis.

In two hours I had done a whirlwind tour of the Daibutsu, the handsome hilltop Hase Kannon Temple with its thirty-six-foot Goddess of Mercy statue. On the climb up, commanding a breath-taking view of the sea and nearby Bozo Peninsula, you see hundreds of small figures of *Jizo*, the patron saint of small children, pregnant women, and travelers, dressed in their little red bibs and hats. I was told once that since Japanese can abort up to the eighth month, their want for boy children being so great, far more *Jizo* than the nation admits are dedicated to unborn souls of unwanted children, a sad but likely true statement.

Today the fresh yellow chrysanthemums and lighted heavy white candles ablaze make one's imagination run wild with observer's grief. This nation is dotted with *Jizos,* all over the landscape in many sizes, all the same shape, many of stone, many hundreds of years old. Perhaps the *Jizos* are a fourth photo symbol, joining the Buddhas, tori shrines, and the chrysanthemum—symbol of the Emperor's family—in this mysterious land across the sea…under a rising sun.

~

Is it lack of roots
That gives me
To traveling?
Or traveling
That gives me
Lack of roots?

Iniri No Tako Matsuri

Iniri Kite Festival

...a low, thick white cloud sent
tendrils of wispy blue-white smoke heavenward,
another offering to the seven angry gods, no doubt.

It was the magic of a brisk, windy, kite-flying day that sparked me to venture out into my previously unknown perimeter of the Sumida River.

We *geijins* rely weekly on wonderful English-speaking press organs —the *Tokyo Journal,* the *Tour Companion,* and the *Tokyo Weekender*— to know where and when monthly festivals and events take place.

On this particular weekend, a tiny boxed event had caught my eye on the calendar page: "Iniri Kite Festival, Iniri Buddhist Temple, near the Washi paper capital of northwest Tokyo, Ochiai...just a fifteen-minute train ride out northeast of town on the Tozai Line." *Washi,* or literally "Japanese paper" is top-of-the-line paper for origami and kites, and very beautiful in its plethora of dazzling color and designs. You can feel the texture of the paper resulting from the pounding, pressing, and processes, from fibers to the imperfection and often transparent purity, and loving hands that make it.

The Tozai runs beyond the Yamanote Loop and is uncharted territory for many foreigners. Why? Because beyond that zone, the English subtitles cease to exist!

I have always been fascinated by kites, by their freedom, perhaps, but mostly by their grace and beauty. In Japan, kites are truly singular works of art.

I did not know if this annual kite festival was one of flying kites, racing kites or displaying kites, but I knew that most of the artists' crafts I saw or purchased were indeed ones-of-a-kind, and therefore great personal treasures to the owners. This day I would not be disappointed in my fascination. I wanted to come away having purchased wee, hand-painted kites I could treasure forever.

Emerging from the green and white train on the south platform, shortly before noon my Monday off, I felt I was descending into a miniature Disneyland! Lanterns and plumes of artificial silk blossoms festooned the streets of Iniri on both sides. One had only to follow the throng. I was conspicuously outnumbered by grandparents accompanying excited toddlers. Was this a child's event, I began to wonder? Had I stumbled into a day for the youth and not the spectator sport I expected to find?

But swept along by the crush of people, I soon felt very inconspicuous. Great canopies and stalls lined the streets for blocks. There were hawkers with everything from corn-on-the-cob to squid and octopus on sticks, great fish-kabobs, cotton candy, and caramel apples. Absent only to an American were the pregnant bouquets of balloons! But, after all, today was a day reserved for kites!

Suddenly, the crowd began to ascend a very steep and narrow stairway leading to a small, solitary temple, lonely on its hilltop setting. Surrounded by homes and apartments, it looked so forlorn, with an unusually small garden. The people ascending seemed to be honoring the crowd descending from the top, while clutching their new kites to their breasts in reverent silence

Those going up with me were carrying last year's kites, some large, some small, some very worn, some still new, all destined to be replaced. So, that was the secret of today, I suddenly realized.

At the top, they were greeted by two young temple girls, their bright orange sarong skirts and cummerbunds encircling their thin waists and lithe bodies. Thick, tight braids trailed down their backs. The host of temple girls bustling about here were as cloned as the New York Rockettes. I wondered what vows of chastity and unity they took to be among these chosen few we see at each religious site?

Equally chaste and somber, twice as handsome and mellow, stood a young, priestly, male attendant with a basket on a handle, accepting the coins from the pilgrims who gave up their kites.

And then! The kites were fed into a rather impressive pyre at the foot of the altar, where they burned in a low, thick white cloud that sent tendrils of wispy blue-white smoke heavenward, another offering to the seven angry gods, no doubt.

So this was what it was all about! Kites, another earthly symbol of good fortune, along with brooms, bamboo stalks, bowls of beans, cakes of rice, cookies with almond centers that the most superstitious Japanese embrace, were being traded in today at Iniri.

Pushed along by the throng, which had swelled enormously in the time it took me to pass slowly and absorb the energy and exuberance of the street fair and vendors, I took my place in line to mount the temple steps. I passed the attendants of a fine altar there with a significant low bow of respect. They waved me through disgustedly as if I had already paid my dues, because I did not step to the altar and throw any coins. I approached the vast array of tables beyond, full of *new* kites that were on sale this sunny, festive day.

What met my eyes next simply amazed me. There were categories of kites from which to choose, though the mainstream of art themes ran familiar to what one would expect in this culture. Store owners bought kites that reflected their identities: fish market men bought giant *koi* leering from behind scurrilous and exaggerated whiskers, young adolescents bought fierce samurai faces jumping off the kite paper, demure young women giggled over selections of gorgeous geisha portraits, and for the grey population were traditional Kabuki heroes, Fuji-san landscapes, and famous artist's landscapes confirming centuries of traditionally acceptable art—the maples, the iris, the pond lilies, the angry seas.

The artist/vendors worked as they sold, with their large *shodo* brushes tactfully slipping over the tightly drawn surfaces of pre-formed kite bodies. Their concentration impressed me, making change with one hand, their eyes never leaving their creation as they continued to work. And their brushes flew deftly. The prices they were getting for their art was admirable, some medium-to-large kites going for as much as ¥10,000-13,000, ($80-100)! The price of "good fortune" was indeed very good.

I settled for two very small kites of Kabuki faces, in tiny packing boxes, to give as *omiyagi* (souvenirs) to my theatre-loving daughter and son-in-law. The Kabuki bright colors and strength were magnetic in their appeal. I told myself that some day I would return and spend more of my fortune on my good fortune, when I could afford it!

As I was leaning forward to appropriately "ooh and aah" at the wares, I became aware of a growing audience. In eye contact, I let the locals know I was having a most enjoyable time, thank you. It seems I was among only four other foreigners this day who had taken the weekday to venture out "beyond the Sumidagawa" (*gawa*: river).

Two were elderly *geijin*—a visiting professor and his wife—the other two were a lovely young mother with her four-year-old daughter.

Our foreign-ness in common, we migrated towards each other after watching the pilgrims pull the thunderous cord on the temple bell, clap to get the gods' attention, say their prayers, toss coins in the wooden grate box at the altar, and leave to be swallowed up in the lunch crowd below us.

Taking refuge on a rock wall in the shade of a magnificent magnolia tree in full bloom, we quickly struck up a conversation. The older couple were from Connecticut and the professor was privileged to be doing some grant research at nearby Tsukuba Science City. They left quickly after consuming their vegetable pocket sandwiches and the last of their coffee.

The young mother, Margaret, to whom I was quite drawn by her sad eyes, was with her daughter, Megumi. Margaret was the spouse of a Tokyo University fellowship student, both from Great Britain. Unhappily, coupled with her cool British reserve, she suffered severely from the isolation so common to corporate and student wives, compounded with raising a young child in such a foreign world as Tokyo. As a foreigner, if one is not attached to a church home or national club, opportunities to communicate or commiserate with your peers are relatively nil.

I truly felt sorry for her as I extolled the merits of my personal affiliations. It was small comfort, I could tell.

I suggested this beautiful young lady seek a cooking class, a language class, or the cultural classes offered by each and every *Ku* within the megalopolis, and ended my brief encounter by taking her picture in front of the stage beside us.

Attached to the temple, this stage was a covered dancing platform and had, as a backdrop, one of the most elaborate, larger-than-life wood carvings I had ever seen in my travels. It was a single, deeply etched pink peony blossom, with leaves, framed in an ornate, gold-leafed border. Truly exquisite.

I look at that picture to this day, at Margaret and her child, and I see the "lonesome" in the woman's eyes. And I remember that when that photo was taken, I had been far too busy then to ever know "lonesome" in Japan. In creating a new life, I was being busy about being busy. I had not known loneliness.

I would later write in my diary:

Alone is a neon word
Written on the back of your eyes;
It jumps out when you least expect it,
And catches you by surprise!

Heading home to the station later, watching an orange, smoky sunset in the distance, twinged by kite-tail smokes and incense tendrils in the trees, I offered up a silent prayer for that young mother and all the other *geijin* lonelies abroad this day.

~

Colored carp kites
Eight-foot giants
Flying in formations
of 3-5-7
In early April winds
from the southeast;
A touch of vibrant color
Punctuating a field of winter
Turning into spring.

I had yet to convince myself: I was not going to be able to read this, so figure out the system or simply go home hungry!

Wrapped processed cheese looks the same in any country, but it could be toothpaste you're seeing. And you could find super glue in a tube identical to a Mint-O-Dent toothpaste. To me, they all looked the same!

One day, I made it to the counter with a jug of laundry bleach, only to be rescued by a delightful high-schooler wishing to practice her token English on me: "You know this toilet Drano?" she said politely, blushing.

I wish I had kept a list of the countless purchases I had to *gomi* (put in the trash): table salt and white sugar looked the same to me in cello wraps, the difference learned when I got them home. Since *shio*—salt—is pronounced "she-o", and *sato*—sugar—is "sah-toe," one could see how even a brave inquiry could net the wrong product. Baking powder, soda, and flours were all chancey, although I soon discovered flour and batters came in paper bags, not clear plastic. I bought the popular *mirin*, a sweet cooking *sake* and frequent substitute for sugar, thinking it *su* ("shoe")—vinegar—one word I quickly learned.

Products pop up in eateries, and I was always a good sport eating out with my students after classes. The usual *geijin* mistake happened the day I mistook *wasabi* for guacamole and, surrounded by my young English students, nearly expired in a popular restaurant. *Wasabi* is a mega-ton green horseradish, reconstituted in squeeze-tubes and mixed with soy sauce as a *sashimi* dip. With beads of sweat appearing immediately along my brow, I thought I was going to pass out right there on my silk pillow. (To get a flavor for this scene, one must see Tom Selleck in the movie, *Mr. Baseball*.)

Happily, vegetables are vegetables and fruits are fruits. And luckily, had it not been for the user-friendly butchers who have tailored their showcases for the shoppers, I would have been at a total loss in the meat department. Under the fierce, bright fluorescent lights, all cello-wrapped meats pale to the same color within hours. Meat labels carry a very clever logo stamp—pictures the size of a postage stamp—of pigs, chickens, cows, thus making drastic errors of little consequence to the buyer.

For lack of large refrigerators or freezers in their tiny apartments, most women shop on a daily farm-to-table basis, and individual portions were the standard. You can buy a four-slice loaf of bread, mini-cartons of four or six eggs, and pints and quarts of milk, great for the single apartment dwellers.

I always perused the fish department with great expectations. "Catch of the Day" takes on new meaning in Japan. Live fish, lobsters, squid, and octopus are available in most major department stores. It is, in fact, a delicacy to serve a live fish as *sashimi* with the eyes still blinking! I was awed at the seemingly unending variety the waters of this archipelago offer up on a daily basis. Many prehistoric shapes and infinite sizes stare up at you from beds of green plastic, or wriggle in fresh sawdust beds, anxious to go home in the housewives' net shopping bags.

One very important reason families shop nearly daily, besides the storage space and refrigeration problem, is that everything that cannot be carried home on the train through the rush hour crowds must be delivered by the store at a fairly substantial fee. Most of the people in Tokyo do not own cars for transporting their own goods, although taxi cabs are an expensive alternative. Quickly becoming more popular were stores offering delivery service. I'd seen their carriers pick through the narrow streets in little mini-pickups with tarp tops, or on motorbikes or bicycles piled seven feet high with parcels—truly an art of balancing in itself.

I had to arrange to be home to personally take delivery, of course. When I purchased my china cabinet, air conditioner, futon, and gas range, I arranged to be home to personally sign for them. There was always an air of American Christmas when that happened, but in this new land, I really wanted to be there, and the reaction of the native delivery man to a *geijin* in Gottano was worth it!

I grew up in Portland, Oregon, where, in the late forties, the entire basement of the Meier & Frank department store was devoted to small, kiosk marketing similar to those of Japan today. I went there regularly with my mother to visit "Aunt Phrona" who ran the carrot juice kiosk. Perhaps with a bit of nostalgia did I become a frequent visitor to the "basement worlds" in Japan.

Major department stores in the heart of Tokyo can plunge you in one escalator ride from the first floor of French perfumes and lingerie down into a noisy carnival of individual vendors hawking their wares and out-yelling each other ten hours a day. Colorful, rotating *sushi* bars, bean paste candies in the making, succulent hot noodle soups in carry-out cups, and dozens of individual culinary delights compete for your attention. Meier & Frank was never like this! The kiosks are adorned with *noren,* little short curtains with colorful painted symbols, like European Guild banners, depicting their wares. Each season, appropriate silk flowers adorn the lattice ceilings that mask outrageous amounts of florescence, turning whites to garish shades of purple.

I felt that the magic of department store markets was the air of authenticity among the vendors, bringing countryside, curbside, and dockside into the basement, all under one roof. Regardless of the often-notorious weather outside, one can be kept spellbound by the carnival atmosphere. These were not just store employees marketing, they were native folk hosting their very own creations.

In most instances, the stations appeared consigned to the retired, elderly population, who have vested out of their lifetime companies but found themselves on pensions not always adequate in one of the world's most expensive countries. After some thirty years, they seem caught in the hideous dilemma of waiting out the ten-year gap until their national Social Security could kick in at age sixty. These delightful, sage citizens discharge satisfying part-time jobs in basements of enchanting, underground Tokyo. There they perform perfunctory daily tasks to the pleasure of millions of onlookers.

Each vendor wears aprons, headbands or head scarves, and there is always a Renaissance-like, festive hubbub that is very contagious as major stores try to outdo each other. The visual and olfactory overload sets your mouth watering, and it's well worth any tourist's visit as I discovered.

I delighted in the costumes they wore, the tasting bites they offered, and of course they seemed eager to watch a foreigner react to their delicacies. To my surprise, I loved octopus and squid but I hated kettle fish; it grew in my mouth with every chew. Little did I know the Japanese chew on it for hours, much like we enjoy beef jerky, or dogs their rawhide bones—come to think of it, it resembled rawhide!

Traditional *udon dashi* soups had a smell and flavor I never could tolerate. Large, soggy, bread-like noodles floating in strong fish stock forced me to decline, with an *Ei, onegai shimasu.* (No, thank you!)

The Japanese are masters in displaying, packaging, and wrapping their products. Sometimes the goods are much too pretty to disturb. Cookies, crackers, and candies come in tin containers that are veritable keepsakes. Origami paper craft and silk scarf *firoshikis* enfold cakes, fruits, even a cold fish! There are certain colors for certain occasions, certain styles of ribbons and bows: it's a scientific art of penultimate correctness.

Everything is a potential "gift" and the Japanese are the greatest of gift-givers. They always seem to be celebrating a holiday; gift-giving and out-giving others can become a very stiff financial burden if you get caught up in it. *Omiagi*—gifts—are essential to most homestays: the visitor must come bearing a gift. I usually chose fresh flowers, a safe choice if you do not know the hosts well. Of course, liquor is always welcome.

The Japanese were not satisfied, for instance, with copying America's Valentines Day *per se*, giving chocolates and roses in a really big, Hollywood-style fashion. They went on to invent "White Chocolate Day," one week later! On this day, giddy young women of the country can give candy to the dashing young "salarymen" in their offices, often anonymously, but nonetheless to the delight of the huge chocolate industry!

The Japanese are also quick to admit they celebrate just for the sake of celebrating, and I was shocked my first year to find the Shinto-Buddhist nation totally caught up in Christmas with lights, Santa Claus, music, and reindeer; Easter was a true rite of spring. Sanrio Company, Japan's equivalent of Hallmark, makes cards, wraps, pencils, pop-ups, cute little gift-y things right on down to book bags, hankies, and clear umbrellas. Frogs, puppies, snub-faced ducklings, and kewpie-like faces with enormous round eyes are practically national symbols.

Where else but in Japan?

Hitsuyona Mono Kanarazu Motte Ikukoto

Take With You What You Cannot Do Without

I sighed in a wave of pleasure.
The elevator of my mind had suddenly hit bottom
and I was truly enervated the entire rest of the session.

There is simply not enough reverence paid to hairdressers in this world. The old American saying, "Only your hairdresser knows," is almost scriptural to me when I recall how much I took mine for granted—the level of trivia we traveled into each other's confidence, my hairdresser and I.

One day in my first October, I looked in the mirror and lamented how much my hair had grown already. I thought casually to myself, "Uh huh, guess I'll go get my hair cut."

But my beloved hairdresser was over four thousand two hundred miles away! The sudden thought of having to communicate my urgent needs and desires for a decent cut to a foreigner left me paralyzed.

First of all, Japanese women do not wear American short-short styles and I had come abroad with a fairly traditional "Chris Evert" layered, shag cut with deep sideburns, and full bangs to cover my distinctly high, Norwegian forehead, about which I was very self-conscious.

Now, how to convey all of the above in a quick game of embarrassing charades led me to a second degree of paralysis! I debated arming myself with a photo. Pouring over the phrase book, I figured my very presence in the parlor would break the ice: "I'm here because I need a hair cut, *honto ne?"* (Isn't that so?) From there on, I was sure we could all point and push and poke and sketch and insist on *skoshi* (just a little bit please) because I surely did not want too much taken off this first time out.

So with this rush of new-found confidence, I took the train to a lovely nearby shopping mall in Kita-Senju where I had spotted a very spacious and antiseptic salon. Eyes stared in military unison when I walked through the magic air door and was met with a wave of that wonderful *"Itarashaii!"* (Welcome!) in precise, soprano, phonograph-like voices from the ladies in the matching baby pink tunics.

What followed was a trip to "Never Never Land." My coat was taken, hung up, and I was given a cup of green tea and a battered, outdated copy of *People* magazine, moth-eaten, and probably held under the counter labeled "For Foreigners Only" in bold print for the novice workers.

I sailed through the push and point and pokes and bangs ordering: *"Skoshi, o kudasai,"* (just a little bit please), ardently, to which everyone within earshot tee-hee'd politely.

And then began the wonderful, aromatic sudsing shampoo, the deep penetrating scalp massage, which has never been replicated for me since Japan.

And for a grand finale which all Japanese stylists throw in for good measure—a quick flick-of-the-wrist *Shiatsu* (neck maneuvering) treatment that gingerly snaps your neck and magically releases three to ten months of stress!

I sighed in a wave of pleasure. The elevator of my mind had suddenly hit bottom and I was truly enervated the entire rest of the session. No verbal banter needed, just total escape from the stress my jobs, both of them at that time, had produced.

I came away with a fairly close resemblance to what I had wanted—perhaps thinner than I would have liked, what with winter coming on—but quite happy with my new hairdresser and myself—the first of perhaps the forty haircuts I would have abroad was a success. Prices, though, were somewhat staggering! A haircut in those days ran ¥3500, about $27. Perhaps that's why they say, "Don't leave home without it"—at least a picture of your favorite Chris Evert haircut, that is!

I recently heard from a friend who has made Tokyo home for some eight years now. She had been to Sweden on a spring respite to visit relatives and returned with "some thirty pair of shoes, innumerable undergarments, and a lot of bauble jewelry."

At first aghast at her numbers, I was reminded of the discomfort and angst at having to clothe myself in this diminutive society. When store clerks saw me coming at them with an inquiring face, they would size me up quickly and start shaking their heads *"Iie, iie, iie."* (No, no, no, we do *not* have your size.) Our sizes, with few exceptions, are simply *not* to be had in all of Japan.

One of the two garments I brought home, in fact, was a lovely pair of wool dress culottes that Tsuneko purchased for me at an exclusive women's apparel shop at an exclusive price I would never have paid—"a small Christmas gift," she said, probably custom-made from a shop called Ample Japanese Women, Inc. The second (still my most cherished dress shirt), was handmade for me by the tailors, my beloved Harashimas, who lived below me in my Naka-Megura apartment my second year abroad.

They embroidered my initials into the left sleeve, stitches of love sewn in next to my heart.

Despite all warnings in the travel books, I had gone abroad with only two pair of sturdy shoes, (I wear a size ten and a half, unheard of on the Asian market), a mere month's worth of pantyhose, and certainly what I thought were ample undergarments to get me through from one trip to the local laundromat to another. These just didn't last since I had come not planing to stay more than a year.

In a little over a month, after thirteen autumnal monsoons, my walking shoes had become so offensive to my keen sense of smell that I had to talcum powder them regularly. Something akin to mildew/foot rot had beset the innersoles. On a get-away trip to Seoul, Korea, in November, I indulged myself in some purportedly black-market Nike look-alike tennis shoes that became my long-distance shoes. And I carried my trusty black patent leather dancing shoes in a bag wherever I went, to change into when I arrived for a formal appointment. Worked for me!

I would like a hundred yen for every hour I spent pouring over proportion and size charts on the backs of nylons, stocking, socks, panty hose or briefs packages, deciphering the LL, XL, XT, ML, and all other attempts at acronym sizes, trying to find pantyhose to fit me! I was soon to discover, of course, that Japanese XLT—extra-long-tall—made it up to about mid-thigh and there they began to bind in an excruciatingly painful manner. They still lacked about eighteen inches from fitting my large boned, five-nine frame! It was hysterical. Even if they had been tall enough, I believe they never would have fit the pounds I was packing in those days. So the old "Don't leave home without it" soon came to mean "bring about forty pair of economy panty hose."

I never could find a brief that would fit my hips, soon firmer from the miles of walking, but still too ample for Japanese garment makers.

In the middle of my second and record-breaking winter, Tsuneko once more came to my rescue with a wonderful flannel-like, ribbed pair of long underwear, like our long johns, which saved me through January from catching a fatal bout of winter pneumonia. I brought them home for a keepsake—more from my fictitious Ample Japanese Women, Inc. God bless them, whoever they were.

In late spring of my second year abroad, my beloved, permanent hair dresser, whom, I had befriended at a language school, Arden Yamanaka, screeched at me over the phone, "Don't you dare buy an over-the-counter-product from here!" I was going exceedingly grey at the temples for a forty-eight-year-old, and in my despondency had thought I would "hit the bottle" and surprise him and color my hair before I traveled to his high-rent salon in Omotesando for my six-week regular trim and style.

Assenting to his advice, I waited. When I arrived at his posh new beauty school on Saturday he said," You simply must not use a Japanese color or toner on your hair; there is only one shade in Japan: shoe black! You will be so sorry." So the dear man cleverly designed a fresh, short, spring cut that blended into my salt and pepper sideburns, and next trip home, I was very careful to "not leave home without it." My six months supply of Nice 'n Easy Clairol was zip-locked safely into heavy-duty baggies to prevent any customs check tragedy and spill.

We take so very much for granted in America—our personal hairdressers, who put up with our driveling rhetoric throughout a twelve-dollar haircut, right down to the thousands of personal product choices and goods made available to us at very affordable prices, *honto ne?* (isn't that so?) Salon sultans listen to us and commiserate with us and for us, and become fast friends— I now missed them in a very special way.

America, God bless it.

Ifuku Koromogae

The Mystery of the Mothballs

Here was "koromogae," *where on one precise day, this homogenous society carefully lays up its winter clothing and changes, on command, to summer garb!*

As I stepped onto the train from the sparsely populated Gotanno platform mid-morning in early June, I stretched on tiptoe to catch a glimpse of Fuji, mutely silhouetted through a pall of pollution. A faint tinge of mothballs curled my nostrils.

I thought this was a rather peculiar odor to spark my still sleepy brain, in light of the fact that Japanese rarely wear perfume, never have a distinct body odor, and never emit human gases in public. I wondered to myself, "Why on earth do I smell mothballs? Did someone just take their grandmother's kimono out of the chest to go to a funeral today?"

I was not far off with that surmise. What struck my eyes in the next few moments was a most startling and profound visual, proof to me that after ten months I was truly starting to absorb the cultural changes and manifestations at a subconscious level.

Men, women, and students on this train to the city were observing a national event known as *koromogae* (change of clothing) where on two exact days each year—once in June, as I was seeing now, and once in October—this homogenous society carefully lays up its winter clothing and changes, on command, to summer garb and vice versa. For all I knew, these were proclaimed in the headlines of the *Mainichi Daily*—literally the "Daily-Daily".

So into mothballs now went the wool suits, jumpers, pleated skirts, vests, and blazers, forever in winter/spring shades of black, navy, dark browns and occasional deep or olive greens. Out of the mothballs came their summer lightweights, pleasant pale blues and checks for the young ladies, navy cotton slacks and short-sleeve dress shirts for the boys, beiges and browns, tans and pungent olives, and often hideous yellow-greens for adult men and women.

Pre-schoolers and elementary students darted about in the briefest of shorts, held by suspenders for boys, and pinafores with pockets for the girls. Matching hats with chin-straps, back packs and book bags have suddenly gone from wool and black leather to cotton twill, navy blue, and an occasional cheerful, shiny red! I thought, "The garment industry must be orgasmic over this guaranteed, bi-annual, human metamorphosis!"

I learned later that, indeed, the garment industry is mammoth and holds a tight monopoly on the design, fabrication, and marketing of the innocuous and regimented school uniform codes, from nursery school age right up through high school. Recently, however, the competition for fashion monopolies and setting the trend for more fashionable statements, particularly in all-girl high schools, had opened a frenzy of designer fashion shows, showrooms, catalogues, and government bidding of annual uniform contracts. All this, I expect, set the stage for the unspoken transition upon graduation into a company setting where, once more, uniforms and uniformity will be the norm and expectation.

It seemed to me, for instance, every department store, restaurant, office, and major trading firm had dress codes and uniforms—a society with a muted palette and subdued expectations, wearing subdued colors, even with the coming rites of spring.

I would be told within weeks, as I too pulled out my lightweight spring wardrobe and myriad of colors and cottons to battle the fierce monsoons and humidity, "*Pat-o-san,* women your age do *not* wear pinks or bright colors!" I had drawn audible gasps when I went to town one day with my "hot-o-pinku" skirt and dress blazer! When the Japanese had regained their composure, I was given to hear whispered, "*O-geijin-wa…*"(Foreigners! What do they know?)

Mothers, in their beehive of activity showcasing their offspring, send them off to schools with *the* most attractive uniforms, often at great personal expense and sacrifice of time. A uniform, for instance, might include such showy trademarks as embossed medallions or logos on the blazer pockets, shoulder badges, insert blazer pocket handkerchiefs, rolled, pleated, or fluted neckties, and, of course, the matching school bags and backpacks, not to mention knee-high stockings with garters or military-sash dressings.

The expense of all this per family, two uniforms each school year, plus dress leather penny-loafers and the numbers of slacks, skirts, blazers, starched shirts and blouses to match, set the average family back nearly a thousand dollars a year, I am told. Costs are supplanted or underwritten by the school system in cases of extreme financial need. Perhaps ties and suspenders do not disappear as easily at night under futons as socks did under my children's bunk beds, but I know that coordinating uniforms is an aspect of Japanese life that must keep mothers on alert six school days a week.

In the course of one weekend, a wand had been waved over this whole nation. As the calendar heralded "summer-come-soon," all the mamma-sans of the nation had been up into the wee hours, much like

Santa's helpers, orchestrating the expectations of their countrymen—laying out clothes to urge and encourage the chrysalis explosion in their "Chrysanthemum nation."

Wakayama, Ho Okimasu

Wakayama, Set Sail!

The great cruise ship rumbles internally as it shifts into high speed.
She shudders and lurches for a moment,
like a great jishin *at sea.*

Today is Tuesday, May the first. This is "Golden Week" in Japan—perhaps the longest, biggest, and all-encompassing holiday enjoyed by the entire nation. The week celebrates the Emperor's birthday, May Day, (a semi-holiday), Constitution Memorial Day, and Children's Day on the fifth of May. At least six wonderful days of relaxation await us. The country literally shuts down and, if possible, natives abroad return home to celebrate.

The Iwamotos have not only adopted me by now, but have called home to Wakayama farms to alert the entire doting family that we're all coming. "Pat-o is here from Orey-gone!" Akitoshi is home from Dallas, on break from his teaching assignment. A true Wakayama homecoming! I'm excited.

I have nothing better to do, except of course celebrate my first real national holiday with a traditional family. And somewhere in all the excitement and preparations, I know that something really big is in the works. I feel honored and curious, and I am simply going along and willing to be surprised.

"Surprise," however, is not the word for it. I am told to pack for a week and be at their secondary sewing factory, not four blocks from my Gotanno apartment, "promptly at 4:00 p.m.," they tell me sternly. I do so in utter compliance.

I threw my rucksack in the trunk of their sleek, white Toyota Camry and off we drove, into the belly of rush hour traffic, skirting the eight-lane Beltline, deep into the south side heading straight for the harbor, of all places.

At dockside of the colossal luxury liner, *Nippon Sunrise*, proud sister ship of a pair of cruise ships in the Nachi-Katsuura Line, our car moves into Lane Five and is quickly loaded and tied down into the hull.

We are going home to see honorable father, Ryoichi Hayashi, and Tsuneko's beloved brothers and families all—and we are sailing there! I am stunned and staggered at my good fortune. Dragging our bags upstairs, a handsome steward escorted us to our own cabin on the first floor. Two sets of made-up bunks in a state room and our own private bath with soak tub greeted us. Meanwhile, walk-on passengers are issued blankets and will sleep in great carpeted halls. I would have gladly sat up all night to sail the eastern shore of Honshu to the tip of this, the largest of the Japanese islands. Happily, however, I didn't have to.

We cast off and set sail at exactly 6:25 p.m.—punctuality being a human virtue in Japan that is never ignored.

"Happy Hour" was celebrated topside starboard at a windowed bar, where we enjoyed the sunset on Tokyo Bay. Sounds romantic enough, but though Tokyo's jumbled skyline is impressive from the water, the bay itself is a misery in stench and water quality—pea soup with croutons, and an air force of hungry, noisy gulls that greeted us from atop what I am told is a future landfill site. Garbage is being dumped inside thick concrete walls to add square meters to the surface and the sprawl of the bustling shipyards. Ugh, the foulness is barely tolerable.

To the port side, ships of every world flag lined up on the horizon like elephants grabbing trunks of another's tail, like conga lines in tandem. All seem very eager to take a number to enter the port of the Tskukiji Fish Market, or greater Tokyo Bay. It was an impressive sight as we cleared the breakwaters; the pulse of Tokyo quieted forty minutes off shore in the fading dusk.

No one has ever been able to tell me where the sprawling metropolitan area of Tokyo ends and Kawasaki joins to even greater Yokohama as we head south. Including Chiba, I can see lights ringing the bay, home to some twenty-five million people.

As we begin to parallel the coastline to the starboard, Yokohama is already but a glitter of tiny twinkle lights, dense but distant. It feels magical and romantic to see the lights come on in the forested hills rising so abruptly from the sea. The density of the metropolitan areas is in stark contrast to the low, coastal villages, now fewer and far between. Great running trains look like pearl strands, circling Cinderella's neckline, their reflections dancing in the darkening sea on this glorious night.

In minutes, the first day of May slipped into a jet-black night. Our great cruise liner rumbled internally as it shifted into high cruising speed. She shuddered and lurched for a moment, like a great *jishin* at sea.

We have truly set sail for Wakayama and a festive air is epidemic among the passengers.

Everywhere there was great camaraderie: seas of smiles and roars of laughter. The buffet was a spectacle, complete with sculptured ice of—can you guess?—a giant carp, of course: a majestic four-foot high symbol of good fortune and protection from angry gods in Japan.

Silver chaffing dishes contained everything from spaghetti and roast beef to aromatic stir frys and great seafood dishes. The steward bussed our table with a grand bottle of white wine. By dessert, the *sake* flowed abundantly.

Then showtime! As we settled into the dark, watching a lit stage not eight feet from our semi-circle booth, an exciting floor show with a Polynesian theme began. The audience roared with approval at the musicians, dancers, tinkling sticks, and bird calls—very loud and pulsating, and at times erotically tantalizing.

What an evening! As we all staggered to our rooms, I was less conscious of the sea lifting us and the pitches and rolls than I was of what an enormous, action-packed day this day had been, for not twelve hours ago I had ridden the train deep into the city, to Naka-Meguro, to interview for what would be my next year's job in Japan.

Now, all I wanted to do was retire my weary body to the lower bunk. Despite the very loud snoring of all three beloved Iwamotos, I slept very well that night.

Wakayama e Kaeru

Wakayama Homecoming

Imagine knowing that all this land,
terraced orchards of blooming mikan *trees*
as far as the eye can see, belonged to your father's father's father!

On Wednesday, May 2, the boat docked at Nachi Katsura, a very tiny village tucked in a tiny inlet. The boat's welcome bell had rung at 6:00 a.m. so I dressed quietly inside my bunk, an artful act even if you are agile, and left the snoring Iwamotos behind. What met my eyes up on deck was something I shall never forget: the sun coming up *over* the ocean!

In all my life as an Oregonian, where the sun sets "into" the Pacific and sunsets are poet's themes and artist's dreams, I had never, ever, been to the east coast nor seen an eastern sunrise over the sea.

The brilliant, already hot May sun was rising out over the stern, but few others were on deck to share the brilliance. An enormous white gold-flame, its eye-piercing sphere filled my entire line of vision. It rose slowly yet steadily over the horizon, off the port side of our sleek vessel, the *Nippon Sunrise.* And I stepped back instantly, surprised by its intense heat, like Shadrack in the face of the fiery furnace.

All too soon, the sun was on its way to the appointed midday zenith, and the fragrant cool morning air from approaching land met my cheeks. Dock time would be an exact 8:05 a.m., and by then high overcast clouds replaced the pristine sunrise I and those few fortunate souls experienced.

Once we tied up, the Iwamotos joined me for a small brunch at a stand-up bar. Akira enjoys every inhalation of his morning cigarettes, and I sip every drop of my strong Japanese coffee—*kohi burakku* (coffee black). The mist and drizzle that will soon dampen our day on the road sets in as we drive off the steel ramps and hit the pavement of this southern tip of the island, Honshu.

To get to the greater Wakayama and the Osaka-Nara area from here requires nearly nine hours of driving along a spectacular coastline punctuated with small lagoons, and neat but antiquated little port towns. The sea is crystalline clear.

My diary notes for the day read, "*Nine hours! We stopped at no less than fifteen Buddhist temples today, little time to enjoy the gardens.*"

The scenery is just simply breath-taking at times because of the spring foliage: iris, carnations, rhododendrons big as garages, and the last of the azaleas in each and every hue. My brain's color spectrum thinks it has never seen so many shades of green on all of God's earth. The frustrated artist in me yearns to capture it all in my mind, and to this day I can close my eyes and see this astounding beauty.

After a rather decadent lunch at a posh restaurant overlooking the sea, we stood leaning into the wind on some great eroded cliffs.

A large sign, in six different languages, reads simply, "The southern-most tip of Honshu." I make sure they take my picture there, leaning, hair tossled. While my eyes squint through the salty moist air to see Shikoku, the fourth main but less populated island of this great archipelago, I realize Shikoku is where dear Akira, most dedicated pilgrim of the priest Kobo-Daishi, will spend his August holiday time, ferrying his car once more and completing the eighty-eight-temple visit in a record three to four days.

But today, Shikoku is encircled with sea mists, and today we are definitely on vacation touring shrines and temples.

As we visited the last of the fifteen temples that day, my left knee began to give way at the top of one steep but impressive four hundred and thirty-eight-step climb. (I counted.) I was forced to work my way down on the seat of my breeches, and in the rain. Most humiliating.

We arrived just in time for a pastel sunset after a rainy day in the rich and fertile valley of the Kinogawa River—Wakayama-ken, and the hundred-year old mansion estate of Ryoichi Hayashi, Tsuneko's delightful, old widower father.

Once a prestigious college professor of history, now retired, Ryochi resides alone on his *mikan,* or "orange" plantation in the enormous, centuries-old stucco, wood, and rice paper home with its cracked tile roof and crumbling courtyard wall. This, I thought, could be a Hollywood location for *Shogun*, the atmosphere replete with a pungent musty, mildew smell, and giant, dusted cobwebs lurking everywhere.

As we drove through the gate of the whitewashed walls surrounding Hayashi Farms, I imagined slipping out of my shoes and walking barefoot with Tsuneko into her childhood. As tears of happiness washed over her beautiful ivory cheeks, I felt the warmth of the homecoming and realized how precious this annual pilgrimage was to this tightly knit family. All the phone calls in the world, no matter how frequent, could not replace her seeing Ryoichi alive, well, healthy, and so happy.

And he is fairly dancing on his slipper toes to see us all, especially his beloved, only girl-child. The hugs are long and enormously touching.

Many deep and deeper bows, and hearty Western, pumping handshakes ensue as I am led through the courtyard of this ancient farmhouse, laid out in an L-shape, against most intimate, shaded, and mossy gardens.

Imagine stepping out to greet each morning under this grand magnolia tree, whose branches must be propped, they are so old and heavy, seeing the rock lanterns and Buddha statue smiling back at you! Imagine knowing that all this land—the terraced orchard of blooming mandarin orange trees as far as the eye can see, producing the sweetest juice—is all yours, and belonged to your father's father's father!

It was in this garden, Tsuneko later told me, where, as a very small child, she was playing on a blanket when a giant earthquake rolled under her and tossed her about, cracking the ground and their giant Buddha.

It is a wonderful reunion. Younger brother, who lives down terrace, just next door from honorable father, came running up the heavily cobbled lane with his shy, slender wife, Toshiko. So this is brother Yoshihiro, a handsome, swarthy, and somewhat rotund version of his father. I note the strong family resemblance and wonderful laugh lines on their faces.

The Japanese reunion is kicked into high gear now and I do not even attempt to comprehend where the conversations are going. Arms around waists, we leave our bags in the trunk and process down the cobbles to Toshiko's lovely living room where she has prepared, probably all day, an enormous homecoming feast.

Built around an elevated pot of bubbling *sukiyaki*, the thinly-sliced beef with the season's vegetables together with tofu and noodles in a sauce of soy, *mirin* rice wine, and *sake*, our smorgasbord comes from every direction. It is heavily punctuated with spirits, wines, *mikan*-juice of course, tall, frosted quarts of beer, and in the end, like a drum-roll finale, the hot *sake* flows.

How proud I am that I can sit Indian-style for hours now, my knees tucked under their handsome mahogany table, and get up and proceed to the tiny *toi-ray* without falling flat on my face. They marvel at my chopstick mastery. They love it that I love everything put before me. And I am more than willing to try it all, particularly some fine pastries for which Toshiko is famous.

This evening has as its guest speaker and place of honor Ryoichi, of course. The beloved father brings out his medal—replete on green velvet in a handsome walnut case—presented to him by the Emperor himself as an outstanding educator of Wakayama-ken, and the forty-five years he gave to the high school as history professor. This historian and religious philosopher has enjoyed his retirement by traveling to China, and recently to Egypt to visit Cairo and the Sphinx.

Six sets of photos are passed around, of him with his colleagues on the tour, and we hear wonderful recountings of his adventure. I marvel at his energy, his obvious bottled, shoe-black hair, and the hint of chin stubble coming out as the night wears on. He is energized by his audience. What a remarkable life this man has led.

The love in the room is contagious, and only when the *sake* finally seizes him, does Ryoichi wilt, about an hour past my own bedtime.

After a wonderful hot *ofuro* bath, I gladly retire up the steep staircase to the guest bedroom, where double *shoji* screens overlook the valley below and handsome *tatami* mats and a thick, traditional bed coverlet await my sleeping time.

Wakayama welcome!

I open the *shojis* to smell the orange blossom air, as I fuzzily sort out the many images and exciting miles today. Soon I have little trouble falling asleep under the influence of the last hot *sake* wine, on my little rice hull pillow.

~

Graveyard reminders
Surrounded by rice fields
A tribute to tradition
Saying: don't disturb family;
And look on us, afterward...
As we first turned this soil
Or fought, that it is yours.

Nara: Furui Jidai No Munogatari

Nara: Ancient Times Recounted

...as my eyes gazed slowly upward they beheld the Todai-ji Temple, housing Japan's largest bronze statue of Buddha, the largest wooden structure in the entire world.

It was now the fifth day of my very first Golden Week in Japan, and already I was having experiences behind the scenes that surely no foreigner would have otherwise—namely, to travel to Nara in the company of Professor Ryoichi Hayashi!

Onward to Nara—ancient, first permanent Japanese capital and cradle to the introduction of Buddhism. Usually mentioned in the same breath as Kyoto, some twenty-six miles to the west, temples and structures from the period 710 to 784 still stand, making Nara a must-see for visitors to this area.

Goose bumps enveloped my body as we neared these hallowed grounds. True to the orchestrations by my host family, yet another family reunion took place in the parking lot of the Nara National Museum!

There, stepping out of their deep tan Toyota was Tsuneko's handsome elder brother, Yoshihiko, and his delicate, lovely wife Naoko, from Osaka. What a wonderful honor to meet them. Yoshihiko, the shy, humble, and rather famous family engineer. Ryoichi is demonstrably very proud of him in his introduction. Under our formal black *kasas* after a warm morning cloudburst, there follows a wave of ceremonial bows and hugs.

Then Ryoichi pointed the way with his collapsed umbrella, like the leader of the band, and the family fell quickly into pace behind him. I walked up front with Mr. Ryoichi, who delighted in my company and flirted as if we were courting. His sense of humor is sharp, his English impeccable. He seemed dedicated to showing me everything of national treasure in one calendar day.

With great burning spasms and sensation, and the barometric pressure in the atmosphere plummeting as we were deluged by torrents of rain, I feared that with the condition of my knee, I might not be able to keep up with my companions as we scurried from place to place at unprecedented pace. So much to see and do, so little time—that was their obvious agenda.

Inside a wonderful open courtyard, surrounded by high, burnt-wood antiquated walls, our first stop was the famous Kofuku-ji temple site, a great dark main hall dating back to 1819. No lights or flashes are allowed here, lest they fade the fragile interior. Our eyes adjusted slowly to the dark, and we strained to see the magnificence inside. Outside again, with now a light rain falling, I delighted in my first glimpse of the five-story pagoda, Kofukuji temple, Japan's second highest, originally built in the eighth century. Its exterior is resplendent in gold. I leaned way back on my heels to look up at its tapered spire, my face tickled by the soft shower.

Awesome indeed is the nearby, smaller, yet more graceful, three-story pagoda dating from 1143 overlooking Sarusawa Pond, where soaking wet children were dutifully getting their pictures taken with grandparents. Some held sticks of cotton candy, others oversized lollipops. Kids *are* kids the world around.

The entire grounds are bare, pounded dirt, nearly concrete in nature, devoid of any greenery or pine needles, much less any litter. Uniformed caretakers, in their navy ballooned trousers, were right there behind us with their conventional pine-whisk brooms to keep it so.

I can see how tens of thousands of pilgrims each week keep the earth beneath beaten down. Today's torrential rains, however, had turned it into a mud slick of rivulets that made walking hazardous.

The grounds became a veritable mud pond before we completed one whirlwind hour touring three great halls which house the National Temple Treasures, the second or third largest Buddhist collection in all the land. My giddy delighted expressions couldn't be contained as my eyes beheld more gold, carvings, ivory, and statuary than I can possibly appreciate in one day. Soon, however, saturated beyond comprehension, it all began to look the same, but I didn't tell that to my host.

This was true of the temples too, as there came a time when they too began to look alike. The Buddhas began to resemble each other, and all that glittered, though gold, began to look like glitter.

Ryoichi sensed my overload, and suggested a lunch break. It was time for the open spaces of the famous Deer Park and some green trees now, despite the rain.

My wonderful, grey Easy Spirit walking shoes were even beginning to "slog-slosh" and I thought my soggy toes might shrink or shrivel with a full day out in this weather. I've been cold and wet all day and began to feel miserable, but everyone else was having such a good time.

At the precisely appointed time, near the great gate of the Toiji Temple, we met up with Hitoko, yet another life-long childhood friend of Tsuneko. Together, we all had a wonderful lunch at a nearby restaurant in the park. My favorite *tempura* dish of fish and vegetables on a platter, almost too beautiful to disturb, was set before me along with pots of hot green tea which I had grown to enjoy very much. Accented with fragile green ferns and punctuated with tiny bright yellow chrysanthemums, my spirits are lifted immediately! In every environment since my arrival in Japan, food is always presented and served in such an artful form—breathtaking, as if the simplest of dishes will appear in an elegant magazine.

Today there are few foreigners here and so I'm the delighted recipient of the finger-pointing banter of several, wide-eyed toddlers crying, "mamma, *geijin-wa*!?" (Mommy, a foreigner!) Very often young children did break out in tears, though I often received a shy smile from one or two of them.

After lunch it was now Akira's turn to set the afternoon pace, one that nearly killed us all! Little did I know that the great temple gate, with identical twenty-four-foot fierce Deva King statues guarding the Buddha, was entryway to still more acres of manicured park grounds, wherein are housed the best saved for last.

With no preparation, I found us queuing up in a long line at a tall stucco entry gate. Very soon we passed through onto a covered, elevated porchway. Stepping innocently to the railing, my eyes fell onto a deep green lawn that must have been two football fields long! As my eyes gazed slowly upward, they beheld the Todaiji Temple, the world-famous Daibutsuden, housing Japan's largest bronze statue of Buddha.

The building itself, dated 1709, is the largest wooden structure in the entire world—though just *one-third smaller* than the original destroyed by fire.

Hot tears just spilled down my cheeks, my breath literally sucked out of me by the emotions I felt. Like Alice swallowing the wrong bottle, I had become reduced to inches high at the foot of an enormous god-throne!

Pilgrims on the long walk out to the temple looked like little ants out there, even at this distance of about two blocks!

I wanted to fall to my knees in reverence. All that seemed missing now was the hedge rows and a few little black and white playing card guards shouting, "Isn't this simply magnificent? Magnificent! Magnificent!"

The family, meanwhile, stood by quietly to take pleasure from my reaction; this *was* the best saved for last! They knew all the rain and chills and soggy feet would be worth this moment. As if they orchestrated this too, the sun then broke through; blue sky and marine clouds bubbled up around the great Temple as if to frame it for my Kodak/Fuji moment. Never can a camera do justice to this climactic afternoon vista, never.

Still a bit numb in defenseless awe, I was eager to visit the Temple, which now grew larger and larger as we approached it. Great throngs followed us down the concrete sidewalks. I entered silently and reverently to stand in the dark, dank interior and gaze up forty-nine feet onto the face of the Great Buddha, lighted only by rows and rows of pilgrim's candles, incense wafting as high as his brow. Those familiar, slanted, lowered lids seemed to hide a Mona Lisa-like smile.

None can compare to this great Buddha of built in 749, not quite as serene as the one in Kamakura, but still commanding deep respect all the same. Repeated damage by fires has caused the head to be replaced twice, plus one hand, though renovations are hard to detect.

It measures forty-eight feet high and weighs four hundred and thirty-seven tons. As a citizen of a country only a little more than two hundred years old, standing in the presence of this bronze giant nearly thirteen hundred years old was indeed humbling.

This Buddha ranks among the wonders of the world, a magnificent pilgrimage event for most native Japanese as well as "*geijin*-tourists".

Particularly impressive are the great inner walls of the Temple, housing heavenly guardians—one stamping a demon—and many goddesses, all there "to protect anyone who approaches the Buddha."

The events of the rest of the afternoon though enjoyable, paled after this. My feet were very damp and tired: I longed to sit down. With the parting clouds, the humidity level rose, intensifying the fiery pain in my knee.

Two main temples remained, housing clay images of four heavenly guardians, and many treasures dating back to 733. I was enjoying seeing so many thousands of Japanese families soaking up their treasure houses and the splendid, lantern-lined walkways. Canopies of pastel wisteria laced the paths with their shadows, providing cool shade.

I soon fell behind the others, enjoying frequent garden benches to sit, sipping a canned ice coffee and enjoying an *o-mochi* rice cake, participating in my most favorite hobby: people-watching.

I was very glad when Yoshihiro called a halt to the afternoon around five. He suggested we ladies sit on the curbside garden wall while they retrieve the cars from the gigantic parking lots some four blocks away. When the two cars drove up simultaneously, we all bolted to get in; a friendly policeman waved us away from the curbside in order to keep the traffic moving.

We were within three blocks of the freeway entry ramp, headed to Kyoto and Yoshihiko's home for a magnificent meal, a late night party and overnight stay. Five of us crowded into the Toyota, I on the middle hump in the back seat.

Akira stayed right on Yoshihiko's trail barrelling into the flow of holiday traffic. Suddenly, not five minutes down the freeway, Tsuneko, in the front passenger seat, let out a blood-curdling shriek.

In the wild conversation with split decisions being made in the next sixty seconds, it became apparent she had come away from the wall where we had waited and had left her black leather bag sitting there. The bag contained not only our return ferry and cabin tickets but also Akira's bullet train ticket, since early Monday business required his speedy return to Tokyo, and we three would ferry back with the car. It also contained what I surmised to be close to one hundred thousand yen, cold cash, or $600-$700, perhaps more.

At the nearest possible exit, we snaked our way back down narrow side streets to the temple grounds, pulled up to the curb, and there, sitting undisturbed in full view of twelve hundred passersby, was Tsuneko's lovely black handbag.

Only in Japan, I tell myself, could this have happened. Only in Japan.

There was much to celebrate that night at happy hour, much drinking and revelry. Tsuneko took a fair amount of ribbing the first couple of hours, teased mercilessly by her family. Her anxiety gave way with short bursts of happy tears. What a lucky lady she was.

Much delicious food was served and consumed at an elaborate Western dining table. My knees were so grateful; I could not have handled a *kotatsu* very well that night.

Professor Hayashi and his wife resided in a very spacious Western-type, two-story home, a far cry from the orange orchards of "home." He is a very highly respected engineer for the Japan National Railway in the Kyoto corporate office, and had recently traveled to Washington, D.C. to accept a large cash stipend and prestigious award for having designed the lightweight, aerodynamic passenger cars that comprise the famous Boston to D.C. commuter lines.

Now was my chance to grill him about the statistics of the impressive, fine-tuned passenger system throughout this entire country. Specifically, my question was: "So, Yoshihiko, how many people are the train cars *really* designed to hold? "

A gulp, a winsome sigh, then an embarrassed smile accompanied his reply, "Our cars are designed to hold one hundred and twenty-five persons comfortably, but we all know at any one given rush hour they may contain upwards of two hundred fifty to three hundred persons!" Third grade math wizard that I was once, I could quickly compute that a twenty-two car train could transport six thousand six hundred people, and the Japanese do it every two and a half minutes! That means the Hibya Line at my poor little burg, Gotanno, could disgorge one hundred and thirty-two thousand commuters per hour at the end of the working day.

Wow. Tokyo's population is over twelve million...yet amazing people like Yoshihiko make it possible to move the Japanese on the rails of Nippon National with an unprecedented safety record around the world.

The evening was replete with wonderful *sukiyaki,* plus a take-out order of *gyoza*— favorite little pork-veggie stuffed pastry pillows—from a nearby kiosk.

Later, from the balcony of my upstairs bedroom, I could reflect on this most extraordinary day looking out over the Hayashi's pleasant garden.

The next day we toured bustling Kyoto proper, and visited Yoshi's palatial corporate offices, and dined in one of the most expensive restaurants in town. That night I finally succumbed to the fatigue of my feet. They were shriveled indeed, and slightly blistered. I stuffed my shoes with newspaper in hopes they will regain their shape overnight and dry out some. Spring in Japan is a test to the watertight shoe industry! I wonder to myself how many pair of walking shoes are in a typical Japanese closet, waiting to dry out. Mine simply sat in my parquet entry way, stuffed with newspaper, doing the same.

Synonymous with Nara and etched on the backs of my eyelids for eternity are the faces of the seven angry gods and perhaps one-hundred thousand happy Golden Week visitors to the most ancient of ancient pathways—pathways seemingly untouched by time—and finally Ryoichi's sheer delight in orchestrating a breathless long day.

~

Japan writes its name
Across my eyelids
in kites...
In bonsai and sakura
And I am awed.

Koyasan: Senzo

Ancient of Ancestors

Like driftwood tossed up from a sea of centuries,
they had found a silent home in this temple of holy men.

Koya-san is the tallest mountain east of Osaka, accessible by the narrowest of busy highways or an impressive cable car, nearly vertical. It is considered the center of the Shingon-Mikkyo, or "True Word" sect of Buddhism, and was therefore saved for our last days with the Hayashi family—a trek to the burial places of revered ancestors.

When you tell people you have been or are going to Koya-san, there is an inspirational "ooh" as if you'd been to The Wall in Jerusalem or to Mecca. And I, still poor miserable *geijin* Christian, would spend a fiercely cold and cloudy weekend trekking around its flat-top forest in my new James Bond overcoat still trying to keep abreast with the Hayashi clan! Here in the holy village of Koya-san, in the dark, dank shade of ancient cedar trees with nine-foot girths, more than one hundred twenty temples carry on tradition, as they have since 816 A.D.

in this holy mountain village dedicated to homage, worship, tourists, holy souvenirs, and occasional coffee shops.

It rained all day long.

We arrived, the Iwamoto clan and I, in two private vehicles, loaded with luggage for seven of us, and were formally greeted at the great gate of a wonderfully preserved temple Hostel Inn. Very early in the day, this place of pilgrimage for the faithful became choked with gigantic, lumbering tour buses. Our cars were passed off to shy valets and for the next two days we were on foot.

Issued navy cotton *yukatas* and *tabis* (white socklets) and sandals, we put our Western clothes into heavily mothballed closets and became cloned guests of the priests and attendants here.

Quiet reigned supreme as our souls and bodies, instantly de-escalated from the brisk pace of Kyoto and Nara. Served a pungent green tea and round plum-filled cakes, we all sat cross-legged in the presence of Ryoichi, and heard from him a lecture on the history of this impressive hideaway, amongst his favorites.

I marveled at the magnificent murals and silk screens that surrounded the walls and graced our gigantic "suite." Outer hallways had a patina that fairly glistened, shiny and slick from centuries of bare feet gone before. As the granddaughter of a master Norwegian carpenter, I thought I saw rounded edges on each and every tongue and grooved floorboard, a wonderful clue to the shuffling toes that had worn them down over hundreds and hundreds of years. Like driftwood tossed up from a sea of centuries, these timbers had found a silent home in this temple of holy men.

Occasionally, I could hear a great muted brass gong, intoning some to prayer somewhere on the grounds. It seemed to come from a great hall north of our rooms, out across a pond that was at least twenty-five feet in diameter, beyond the screened hall from our room. The heavily shadowed pond was alive with croaking frogs and brimming with huge *koi.* Birds darted in amongst the low, drooping maples and azaleas. A green slime edged the shore; thick moss clung to rocks outlining stepping stones that led to the middle of nowhere. And I heard the faint trickle of a near-mute waterfall somewhere in the dark corner where a giant tortoise reposed. It was all too beautiful to consider as reality.

Dinner came on tray after tray, served by a shy, mute inn keeper in a warm brown *yukata* and wide *obi* sash of gold. As we knelt to eat in this, our adjacent suite, with its small altar and *shoji* screens opening out onto still another greater but sunlight garden, there was no conversation. We all seemed content in the safe arrival, very hungry by now, and cognizant of the rules. Other guests, shuffling by in their straw *zori* sandals, never lifted an eye to stare.

This was, in fact, a working hotel, an integral bed and breakfast of sorts, complete with hot baths and soak tubs, providing hours of meditation with the most holy of holy priests. Armies of priests clad in the bright yellow-gold robes scurried silently around the halls, their feet barely touching the ground. Each seemed to have an appointed task, some carrying candles, some trays, some fresh linens. Most appeared very young.

After our sumptuous *tempura* meal of vegetables and rice and much washing down with green tea, we went off single file to the Inner Hall for what seemed to me to become at least an hour of chanting and meditations. Incense makes me nauseous and I was instantly overcome for a moment, particularly on a full stomach. Kneeling on my arthritic knee made me faintish, so I was doubly overwhelmed, but I managed to stay down, shifting frequently to the obvious annoyance of Tsuneko.

When I became accustom to the darkness and candlelight, once again the gold—gold in scores of small statues, gold, gold, and more gold—illuminated only by tiers of great, gooey, dripping, globby candles and their halos overwhelmed my senses. The chanting of the worshippers, male and female, perhaps fifty of them, resting buttocks on heels for an hour, pressed up close to the altar, seemed to be a unison monotone. I dozed and swooned and was brought back to life by a sharp Akitoshi elbow.

When the service was over and the Japanese trailed across the altar to sweeten the cash box with coins and bills, I leaned back towards the curtained walls, sheer gauze layers over velvet red swatches, and watched their quiet procession out a heavy carved door.

Somber and silent...no footsteps could be heard on this great red carpet where I believe two hundred could kneel under the gaze of a slender Buddha.

The priest, behind his snappy black glasses, almost aglow with perspiration on his shiny bald head, gave me a most pleasant half smile and nod of acknowledgment. I felt warmed and welcomed. It was a reassuring moment for me.

Back in our rooms, the Hayashis excused themselves to their quarters, and Tsuneko, Aki, and I dressed for the night in lighter cotton *yukatas,* and in silence.

With body language and a simple finger to his lips, Aki assured me we will continue to be silent until the pre-dawn call to worship. I was so relieved. Anything less would be irreverent under this evening's mood, set by the hour of meditation. I am alone with my thoughts of where exactly I am, where only few but God and I know where exactly that is!

I brushed my teeth in the communal bathhouse where seven faucets and seven mirrors reflect seven clothes hooks on the opposite wall. Garden spiders danced on the cold wooden floors and Japanese style toilets greeted me from behind swinging doors. A small child with her mother entered for her nightly tooth-brushing ritual, spotted me, the foreigner, and shrieked in despair! I flushed with shock, realizing that perhaps, up here on Mt. Koya-san, I was the first *geijin* this child had ever seen.

At some point in the darkness, Akitoshi breaks the silence to whisper, "*Pat-o-san,* do you like it here…amongst the ancient ancestors?"

What can I say but that I am moved and overwhelmed.

All through the night, as the novitiates came and went, I noticed those floors never ever squeaked, but I, in turn, who never have a problem sleeping in strange places, tossed all night. I think I was afraid I might fall asleep and miss something exciting! This place held so much magic for me—perhaps a foretaste of the day to come.

~

slender fingers, small bones…
always catch my eye.

Sugi No Shita No Shizukesa

Reverent Silence Under Koya's Cedars

...families regularly and devoutly honor the memories of ancestors in frequent and ritualistic ways.

As a mountain resort providing an escape from the heat and humidity of the lowlands, this day Koya-san is a bit inclement, to say the least. The cold had moved in during the night and I woke with the comforter tight under my chin in our fine temple beds.

Fifty-three of the one hundred and twelve temples are designed to accommodate visitors. But I believe less than five thousand foreigners a year trouble to make this trip to the highlands east of Osaka. While not especially a photographer's paradise, Mt. Koya was a spiritual experience I shall never forget. Most places forbade camera flashes and the dense cedar forests make natural lighting poor.

When the welcome bells called us at 5:00 a.m., I was hard-pressed to stir, but knew better than to grumble. It is Friday, Tsuneko's day to visit her revered ancestors enshrined here. Today, a miserable drizzle etched the roof tiles and danced in the tortoise pond. I traded a morning shower for a quick immersion in the enormous indoor natural lava rock soaking tub. This warmed my cold bones. I quickly donned the temple *yukata* and hurried to catch up with the clan for morning vespers.

Koya-san is, in fact, the site of an extensive cemetery, and the pilgrims today were here to visit relatives buried in this small mountain village. Gobyo, scarcely three miles across town, is the vast mausoleum of Kobodaishi, founder of these temples and a great teacher of Shingon, who also devised the simpler *hiragana* syllabry for writing Japanese.

Regular ceremonies honoring deceased family members have led the world to the mistaken belief that Japanese worship their ancestors. The religion that the families have, for the purpose of honoring their ancestors, has stayed with that household since ancient times, and often has little to do with their current religious faith. Honoring on or at certain times of the year, Golden Week for example, becomes a time-honored event, much like our cleaning up and decorating of cemeteries.

All in honor of deceased love ones.

Here we were on Mt. Koya, the family regularly and devoutly honoring their memories, in frequent and ritualistic ways. Remembering that this is a nation relying on cremation, here, deep in the womb of these underground mausoleums, are deposited some slight remains of a relative, perhaps a fingernail or lock of hair, lodged here for posterity. The ashes themselves are deposited in a common family burial site along with several generations of that family.

This day, we journeyed down many flights of winding stairs deep into a unique underground temple maze where, in a tiny niche with a keyhole for air space, at a height one would have to stand on their tiptoes to eyeball, we pay our respects and have a brief, whispery conversation with Tsuneko's mother, formerly of Naga-cho.

Days before, we had visited her cremains on the family plot blooming with lilacs, and a stone's throw from the railway tracks, not far from Ryoichi's farm. We took fresh flowers, incense, and *sake*, scrubbed the marble stone, and prayed in silence.

And now we were standing in the presence of her nails and a lock of hair—chosen because they do not decompose with time—in a place where privilege does not come cheap.

For the honor and memory of being here in Koya-san, the family is expected to purchase one of the ornate gold box lanterns at approximately $700 apiece.

While I should have been meditating, I stopped counting at three hundred and sixty-five thousand drawers—the stairways deep, times the rows high, times the blocks deep of this hallway. So many thousands of little drawers are set in the walls, with its low, cavernous ceiling that has since been wired for electricity from times where once upon a time wax candles required hundreds of temple attendants to care for them. It was like something out of Indiana Jones.

As we stood in front of the eight tiers of niches, each five inches wide and ten inches high, palms pressed together, meditating, Akitoshi leaned towards me and whispered, "Do you wish to say something to Grandmother?"

Flabbergasted at the thought, I reply feebly "Gosh Aki...I wouldn't know what to say since I did not know her." He nodded in simple understanding.

At last outside this musty, dank dungeon, I was relieved of my claustrophobia. The grey ceiling had dropped to the treetops now and my handsome khaki trench coat—a birthday gift in January from the Iwamotos' own retail line, since I think they were too overwhelmed with my hot pink one—defied the chilly winds swirling about us, kicking up pine needles. A fog had settled in the trees giving this strange place an ethereal atmosphere. Travelers disgorged from the yellow *Hoto* buses that roared away to acres of empty lots to make room for still more buses thundering in behind them.

In this giant forest of tall cedars, their limbs damp and somber in the alpine air, I was forever falling behind so was able to notice the infinite variety of tombs and memorials. Some plots are fenced, decrepit, wasted, and weakened by time. Some of the stones of the memorials have fallen and are left to be enveloped by moss on this soggy earthen stage. Wooden plots have all but decomposed, altars and headstones, as a lone fence post marks what was probably once there. Except for the busy little concession stands and frequent priestess' stalls where you may buy fresh candles, incense, or wish sticks and fortunes, this whole vast cemetery plot seemed untouched by time. No rejuvenation or remodels here, no fresh green grass. Clothed only in moss, this cemetery is set in time, a time standing still by choice.

Young monks in saffron robes with a propensity for scurrying about, looked to be busy running errands—lanterns to the catacombs, flowers to the graves. This weekend altars would see a lot of fresh foods, bouquets, *sake*, pyramids of apples and fruits, all the adornment necessary to please the ancestors and their memories.

Incense sticks caused bluish wisps upon the heavy humid air. If it were raining hard, we would be under a circus-like canopy so thick daylight resembles a winter dusk, and droplets drizzle down upon us at a steady rate.

Akira was buoyant in his gusto to be here. He led us on throughout the grounds, and as we approached an exit walk, daylight broadened. The forest was less dense and manicured shrubs adorn the barren grounds. This newly carved-out section of the immense cemetery had the appearance of a more Western cemetery in its bold, sleek headstones. Some ten- to fifteen-foot monoliths of concrete and marble, sandblasted deep with single, familiar family names like Toyota and Honda catch my eye. Akitoshi is quick to explain to me that we are in the new "corporate quarter," and only exemplary employees of these "family" companies may be enshrined and remembered here by the company. "No doubt the CEO headquarters," I chuckle to myself irreverently. Somehow the whole concept is coolly unappealing and too calculated to my American mind, cynical about these matters.

I smiled wanly and had no way of communicating my disappointment in the whole concept, which is probably just as well. It does nothing to dispel the silent reverence under Koya's mighty cedars.

Naka-Meguro: Hibya San No Shuchaku Eki

Naka-Meguro: The Other End of the Hibya Line

...winter days without central heating,
every inch of plastic anything in Tokyo was freeeeeezing!

When I moved from dearly beloved Gotanno in late June of my first year to Naka-Meguro to take the administrator's position at Tokyo International Learning Community (TILC,) I literally moved from one end of the Hibya Line to the other—from the northern most bounds of the Tokyo beltline subway network to the southernmost, near Tokyo Bay, at the pleasant juncture of the private Tokyu Line, connecting with nearby Yokohama via the outskirts of Kawasaki.

Suddenly, to be a half-hour from Yokohama and the sea gave me a new vista for respite, just as the mountains had been in Gotanno. A new door opened for this great-great granddaughter of Norske Vikings from the sea, and I enjoyed a real rush in traveling often to the notable

Yokohama seawall just to breathe in the salt sea air—a very economical train rate and mere half-hour express train out of Shinjuku Station.

At the same time, however, being closer to the sea also meant that the humidity escalated, or was it my imagination?

Moving to Naka-Meguro meant moving into the tiny clapboard, second story flat occupied by my predecessor, Lois, the former young administrative teacher. The school board underwrote the occupancy, I paid the rent, and I agreed to purchase her furnishings. This is commonly done when one leaves Japan; garage sales are touted as "Sayonara Sales." Lois had a wealthy Japanese beau, so I inherited some very nice things, particularly the sofa bed, double-layer drapes to keep out the sun, a robotic vacuum that did a great job, and a two-burner gas stove that was worth its weight in gold. I was delighted with it all.

In addition, she left towels, cleaning products, dishes and glasses, and a little antique cupboard just inside the door meant for shoes and slippers. My new abode was all so cheery and native and quaint. The Iwamotos arranged for a moving company in a tiny little van to move what little I had that didn't belong to the language school apartment, but at least I didn't have to go by train, one suitcase at a time. I gave my bicycle and a few household goods to incoming missionaries—a newlywed couple out north of me and, quite by chance, the daughter of an old college chum. It's a small world, after all.

I was hopelessly happy for ten months in this apartment with its paper-thin walls and windows. Here was an older Tokyo, with postage-stamp gardens and dark and narrow winding back streets, occupied by very ancient citizenry. And while I was the object once more of curiosity as an isolated *geijin,* I had stepped back another generation into an old urban society. It was magic, so many quaint old neighborhood groceries that I could not get around to them all—wonderful farm-to-market foods that made daily shopping a necessity to enjoy the plethora. It was everything wonderful about Japan.

One of my new colleagues and her husband were furnishing a new apartment and I bought their old but charming round table and two cane bottom chairs from them, also in lacquer black. It made my little black refrigerator look like quite the focal point, and red became my accent color for everything: linens, dishes, pots and pans. On my move the next spring way out west of Meguro, I would leave much behind for the next headmistress of the school, as was tradition.

My most prized possession? A most charming, pregnant, round, red tea kettle that served me well, one I paid a handsome and unheard-of four thousand nine hundred yen for, nearly thirty-eight U.S. dollars!

When TILC sought me out with my credentials in Gottano that late spring, they agreed to send me back to the States for not only family time, but for an intense seminar in Colorado having to deal with autistic and special needs children. They were convinced of my administrative skills, albeit after life on the high desert managing a multi-grade school for two years, but in order to justify to parents of offshore companies, embassies, and nationalities sending their offspring with diverse degrees of handicaps, they knew that their new "Administrator" would have to be able to flag some current documentation.

The series of workshops and many exhaustive wee hours of text-book reading in an Aspen condo was their Rx for my "awareness," such that I could handle the projected fall enrollment as well as the delightful staff they assured me would be returning.

With some impressive certification months later, I departed, wearing a green Snowmass tee-shirt I bought at the little airport.

This was such a great arrangement for both TILC and me, for I went jaunting on from there to Oregon to attend summer session at the University of Oregon, a special crash course in multiple handicaps.

I found the coursework there more applicable in a campus setting with real, live, summer school children. The language or jargon for special education and its overwhelming demographics and statistics were really valuable to me. Once back in my hometown, finally, living with a long-time friend, renting a bedroom and bath accommodation, I leveled out my ten-week summer with another two weeks at the center for handicapped children, the Alyce Hatch Center.

Under the tutelage of an amazingly compassionate and sharing veteran staff, I would be able to take on the new job with severely handicapped children of English-speaking foreigners attached to Tokyo, military, and private sectors. *Ikimasho*—so let's go—once more.

In those fast-flying five weeks back on my own turf, I relished spending some time with my own children.

Kari, now a sophomore now at OSU, was in and out of the Redmond (Oregon) Air Center, fighting fires for the Forest Service on the famous Yellowstone fire that year.

Robyn had a home in Corvallis raising two fine stepsons with husband Lehr.

And I was busy getting to know my new daughter-in-law, Christi, very pregnant with my first grandchild! Throwing her a huge shower gave me a chance to see so many friends, and I think I sensed they continued to be fascinated that I had found a niche in a foreign land and was so happy there.

August days are long in Oregon, and I was able to relax and enjoy picnics with corn-on-the cob drooling in butter, staring at lawns dried up in August heat...that's what I loved about summers at home.

There was some distance with my own Number One Son, Bryan. With his first child about to be born, how could I explain to him the intense loss I felt without his father, John, and how much I needed to heal the hauntings of "alone." And so I returned to Japan on August 22, and precious Megan Louise made her entry into the world three weeks later, after my monsoonal arrival back Tokyo, and a second resplendent autumn upon us.

I remember vividly the rather obese, southern Baptist pastor of the church where my little school took third floor residence that year, as he stood huffing and puffing in my doorway one midmorning, surrounded by all my staff, whom he had summoned for the "event."

"Young lady," the dear man announced in his magnificent and theatrical deep drawl, "it seems you have become a grandmother this fine day, and in Japan we call you *obachan*! Congratulations!" *Obachan* is indeed a term of endearment, and even though my four grandchildren since refuse that and call me the Norwegian *"Nana,"* I find *obachan* a well-earned and endearing title.

Though the heartache of this four-thousand-mile separation never went away, I was greatly comforted by reality that we had Megan!

While away, I had sublet my Tokyo flat to Nancy Reed, a young woman coming into St. Paul's Lutheran congregation from Boston, and my friend to this day. My *apato* on Kamimeguro Street gave her a place to land and get on her feet, and eight weeks to job and apartment hunt. She moved out the very day I returned to Tokyo, leaving fresh milk and ice cream in the fridge, with fresh roach traps set out. It was just the greatest homecoming, like going once round the revolving door and never having been gone: home at last!

All too quickly the small sofa bed I collapsed upon from jet lag was little comfort in the extraordinary August heat and humidity, portending the wake of many monsoons about to hit. A reality check reminded me

I had, in eighteen short hours, transcended once more into life in the ever-turbulent world of my beloved Tokyo.

There were some curious elemental problems with this second-story apartment that took a bit of getting used to. Clapboard construction allowed light, sound, fumes, wind, bugs and heat to enter through cracks in the house; the more frequent the earthquakes, the wider the cracks! I stuffed newspaper into the obvious ones. Come winter, getting more clever now, I sought the Japanese equivalent to spackling and putty and did away with some major wind corridors.

In a typhoon or great monsoon just off Tokyo Bay, the building seemed to pitch and sway, which I found a bit nerve-wracking. In addition, the walls were ever-so-thin and the single-pane windows, frosted for privacy throughout, were poorly set. They made a terrible clatter in the frequent winds, and in a great *jishin* the windows took up the vibration with a vengeance. In my year there, my apartment withstood many, many substantial bouncers and rollers.

Every sound from neighbors below and in all four directions could be heard: one very aggravating barking dog, many screaming children, and loud televisions and radios, just to name a few.

The rather annoying, whirring electric sewing machines from Mr. and Mrs. Harashima, the industrious elderly couple next door, kept my floor vibrating at a certain frequency. Since I slept on that very floor, I vibrated well into the night!

Mr. and Mrs. Harashima were the venerable, honorable, industrious tailors working a handsome little piece-meal operation in the downstairs of their modest home, with a fine garden out the east windows.

At the same time, the Harashimas welcomed me as if I were blood kin to former tenant, Lois. And they took up with me where they left off with her, with sincere tears in their eyes for "Lois-chan-gone"—*chan*, pronounced "chawn", suffixed to a proper name being a term of endearment.

The wall of the Harishima's two-story home and my kitchen wall were adjacent, a breath away, with not one ray of daylight passing between them. The fire hazard of this and nearly every dwelling throughout the Meguro-Ku became very apparent to me that first day back from America. I always knew what they were having for dinner by the smells, and heard their TV every evening.

These wonderful elderly people were, for me, the epitome of my "folks away from home." They accepted my registered mail, kept an eye on my rusty wrought-iron stairway, monitored every footstep up to my door, and gave me full account of any and all visitors. They watched the place when I was frequently away weekends, and habitually gifted me with fruits, pastries, fresh flowers, words of condolence when I was either home late, overworked, or struck down by the heat.

It became impossible over the year to out-give or return their untold kindnesses and friendship to me, a rather common Japanese thing to do. Not complaining about my vibrating sleep or their loud TV was one way, but every time I gave a fruit or bouquet or quart of cold beer at chat time, they were right back on my doorstep the next day with some sort of gift to reciprocate.

When their son had a baby, we celebrated with a drink and shared pictures. When my granddaughter Megan was born, I shared this news when it came by fax, and we plowed through our translation dictionaries looking for key words, like "only son," "first born," "girl child," and now me an *obachan*, grandmother!", cleverly calculating pounds and ounces into kilograms with reactions such as, "*Honto ne!* very big baby." By Japanese standards, everything American seemed big! And the laughter that accompanied it all warms me to this day.

Each morning when I loaded my bicycle basket and prepared to go to work, Mr. Harashima would appear silently from behind his gorgeous twelve-foot rose bush by the porch, bow deeply with his soft-spoken, "Good morning, Pah-to-ree-shya, have a good day," as he practiced his English on me. I deduced he had heard the creak of the iron stairs over his sewing machine, which was always engaged by sunrise with that annoying whirring. His smile would melt an iceberg on the North Sea; his clear eyes fairly danced. His sincerity so abundant, making my heart soar. He was a gentle man with thin shoulders and frame, reminding me of my father's stature. His slender piano-playing fingers turned collars and lapels on thousands of dress shirts each year for the prestigious Tokyu department stores. Within a week I truly thought adoption papers went with the monthly rent I paid. The Harashimas were a substantial part of this whole microcosmic neighborhood.

I had graduated from one little room in Gotanno to two spacious rooms here on Kamimeguro Street, with a two-room bath! A double bath meant one dressing room and a self-contained, tiled *ofuro* on one side, adjacent to my separate sink and toilet area. This was great when I had guests, since each had its very own door for privacy.

Those doors did not add up to any insulation in the depth of winter, however. Fierce winds off Tokyo Bay roared under, through, and around every door and window.

One time I emerged from my morning hot shower into my lavish kitchen to hug the tiny portable heater. Steam rolled off my body like a movie scene at the Turkish bath. Only then did I feel sorry for myself for the complete lack of central heating, normal for Japanese apartments, a lavish luxury saved for the wealthy.

To this day, I sleep with the windows open year-round and seem to thrive in winter, my body acclimated so well to the situation…but it took some getting used to.

From the front door into the kitchen-dining room was a long narrow *genkan,* or entry hall, which I used as a mini-office, housing the wonderful desk and book shelf I found very early one Friday morning in the *gomi-sanrun* (garbage pickup) just a half block away.

My friend Maureen came before school and helped me schlep it home and up the stairs. After two coats of high-gloss black paint, someone's throw away became my pride and joy!

It is totally acceptable to go through street garbage piles in the early dawn on a first-come, first-serve basis. We *geijins* can talk all night of our accumulated treasures, not the least of which was my life size stand-up poster of Sean Connery and Dustin Hoffman from the video store alley.

My great kitchen area was about twelve-foot square with a vaulted, unusually high ceiling, a blessing to my claustrophobia. The living room was carpeted wall-to-wall in a new, easy-care grey. It had one wall entirely devoted to sliding, tastefully muraled *shoji*-screens, which concealed a deep closet space which would hold my wardrobe on hangers, futons and bedding, books, shoes, ironing board, vacuum, empty luggage, and stacks and stacks of underwear and sweaters. It was a wall by day and cupboard/closet by night—ever so functional.

All I had to do on laundry day was open the full glass panels of the north and east walls and hang my clothes out on a marvelous laundry line system installed by the landlord, fastened permanently to the eaves. I quickly found that if I soaked the sheer curtain panels of these two patio-door windows and hung them back up wet, the air-conditioning effect to the entire living room was both fragrant and efficiently cool on unbearably hot days and nights. Probably drove the temperature down ten degrees too.

A wonderful garden below the east window, where I often hung over the back of my sofa bed to wistfully enjoy an evening breeze and watch the elevated trains to Yokohama just a block away, had dwarf iris, a *mikkan* orange tree, camellias, lilies, and a great assortment of colorful rock flowers. I don't believe over the months that the elderly couple minded the silent *geijin* audience. The fervor or reverence with which they tended the plants was a spectator sport. Lilliputian flower pots were delivered a finite mist as they hand-cared for each and every inch of the perhaps eight-foot square plot. But in Meguro-Ku, this garden was palatial.

In the spring, that elderly gentleman across the way was suddenly confined to bed with some sort of malady for which his bouts of coughing either woke me in the early morning hours or kept me awake; I finally had to resort to earplugs. Weeks later, the coughing stopped. Harashima-san never told me. I never asked. But one night all the ground floor windows of the house were opened, every light on, the body laid out, much coming and going and weeping, and I believe I saw a wake taking place.

To the north, I could flip a coin into what was the outside stairway of a working men's dormitory. This is a common arrangement for single male workers in big cities. Shifts of beleaguered men came and went regularly there, watched pornographic movies round the clock, and hung their plumbers' and carpenters' balloon pants and tabi-toe stockings out to dry under their eaves.

The apartment wedged between the garden spot and dormitory was yet a newer home, spawned up amongst the post-war wooden clap homes, with fine stucco exterior and tile roof, modern *shoji*-screen sliding windows. The couple who lived there had an electronic keyboard and a midget yippy dog, need I say more? At least I tried to keep my beloved Sony tape player down to a cool Kitaro or saxophone jazz, but there are degrees of neighbors the world around and Tokyo was no exception.

Directly south, within reach of my railing and hiding behind an ominously cracked and peeling stucco wall, was the backyard canopy of a great, silent grove of ancient trees that allowed no one to know who or what lay below.

The traditional agrarian farmhouse inside this ominous wall never revealed a sign of life to me. I could hear scrubbing on a cement slab, water being thrown out, and occasionally saw linen laundry on a second story line, but never in ten months did I know the whereabouts or "who-abouts" of the occupants. I enjoyed the spring fragrance of their fruit trees and yellow-gold oleander. And I suppose I enjoyed the tricks my imagination played with my mind of *shoguns* gone before us on this very hallowed ground.

Over the top of that same canopy of autumnal leaves, I was a visible "neighbor" to my fifth and last apartment across a narrow alley. The lady of the house and I became hand-waving friends almost immediately. We first met when I stepped out of the shower on a hot evening and found myself standing stark naked in the window as she was cooking up something wonderful in her rice cooker. I could see right into her lovely kitchen through second story frosted windows, and she could see right into my *ofuro* bathroom! Keeping in mind her perspective, I made sure from then on that when the frosted window was closed and back lighted, I was to either duck down or limit this somewhat intimate sport of "shadow-watching."

The same precautions went for the toilet cubicle and its two walls of half windows, frosted and originally for ventilation purposes. I had to be especially careful in that room because my apartment had the "traditional" Japanese toilet. It resembles a large elliptical urinal raised an uncomfortable twelve inches off the floor, over which you are to step up and squat, facing forward to a porcelain flush handle on the wall.

For a *geijin*, that puts you well up at window level again. So toileting for me became quick-in-quick-out. It was very hard on my back, legs, and bowels early on, since I had been spoiled by a western toilet in Gotanno.

On my very first autumn pay day, therefore, I went trucking off to a wonderful large department store called Tokyu Hands, in Shinjuku, where I spent the handsome sum of around forty-nine thousand yen on the niftiest "conversion kit," turning my hole in the floor into a completely western toilet.

The kit was a self-contained hard plastic toilet that fit right down over the existing hole. Now, not only could I sit in comfort for greater lengths of time, I was down out of sight. And it came with the cutest little knit seat cover for winter days when, God knows, without central heating, every inch of plastic anything in Tokyo was freeeeeezing!

I was able to bicycle uphill to my new school each day, a mere ten minutes away, located on that third floor of the Tokyo Baptist Church. I came to know a fine hairdresser around the corner, I established a bank just three blocks away where they knew me on first-name basis, I found a nearby pub, and the greatest pork *tonkatsu* dinners in the southside, and, best of all, being on the other end of the Hibya Line, I was always assured a seat on empty cars, for the train originated here in Naka Meguro. Going into the great yawning belly of Tokyo on my weekly errands or just two stops away to the crossroads of magnificent Shibuya Station, I was but an hour from my beloved Iwamotos and old Gotanno.

For twenty months, this was *home!*

Shuriken to Kokoru

Darts & Hearts

This scotch-on-the-rocks Scots,
soon to become one of my very dearest offshore friends,
was indeed a bit of a gypsy rascal.

Late in the fall of this second year abroad, it occurred to me I suddenly had a balanced life with real free time. My job as headmistress of a small school, with regular hours, living walking distance from my delightful little Meguro apartment, gave me time to meander and wander the neighborhood in daylight and evening hours. I realized at the same time that I longed for some English-speaking friends and casual conversation

At the Tokyo Learning Community School (TLC) for handicapped children, my teachers included our wonderful Dutch speech therapist, a New Zealand physical therapist—the lone, boisterous, giant, fairly arrogant male, two Japanese assistants—incredibly polite and adorable, and two Americans—one with such a heavy New Jersey accent that an all-day exposure set my teeth fillings on edge!

I loved them all and depended completely upon them, as I ran the organizational track all by myself, tucked away in an office with a patio-view of the majestic Fujiyama, spending most days on the phone, buried in paperwork, extensive files, and correspondence—my forte.

Although I enjoyed their company, the camaraderie, dynamics, and the hysteria that sometimes accompanied being headmistress of it all, we were all business, all about the kids, our charges, and very little time for social talk. A true balance with some social time just was not there. And at the end of the day, my entire staff went off home to their spouses, posted offshore in their exciting Tokyo world, a home, dinner, nannies, and children to attend to. And here I was again—alone.

Eating alone was now getting troublesome and heavy, words like "forlorn" and "remote" had entered my head by the back door. The truth was that I was desperately isolated. Here I was, back in Tokyo, a long train ride from Gotanno now...moving up and onward each new autumn always seemed a bit daunting. Making friends in this new Meguro neighborhood seemed a bit of an overwhelming chore.

My stunning blonde staff colleague, Maureen, the one without the Jersey accent, gifted in working with my severely autistic children, and whose husband was a foreign journalist, suggested during one lunchtime over a hot pot of green tea, "You should join Arty and me at the Tokyo British Club some night! It's just one dark alley off the Shinjuku line; I'll draw you a map. We play darts and the fish and chips are to die for!"

Walking alone into a club of any sort was not my nature, I assure you, but truly: good fish and chips had a strong draw. So one night I pocketed the map and found myself trekking up that dark alley that paralleled the train tracks with a high, safe wall, where some questionable night spots were also open for business.

All too soon I spotted a simple and innocuous sign pointing up some outside stairs to a second story "Tokyo British Club."

What hit my senses, after I passed the umbrella and coat entryway and opened an inside door, was soft Celtic music, strong cigars, and laughter. I love cigars, and the laughter was instantly warming—good, English belly laughs and raucous, wholesome noise. The Queen's English and some very loud Scottish brogue hit my ears…and I was smitten as the bartender motioned me to come sit at the barstool counter.

All men, this early in the evening, felt like the Queen's Navy of big brothers! I was asked to introduce myself, labeled immediately a "token Yank!" and somebody two stools down bought me a short, iced pint of deep amber ale. I swiveled around and saw a dark corner with card players and two gents throwing darts, a game that was soon to tease out my every last ounce of competitiveness.

Sir Bryn, we'll call him, fictitious to protect his aging innocence, was sitting at the curved end of the bar, looking very overheated and uncomfortable in his seasonal but heavy tweed suit jacket. He eyed me with a twinkle I shall never forget in riveting small blue eyes. Wind tossed, coarse hair dusted his forehead to balance out his fine, squared Scottish jawline. Quite handsome in a roguish, rascally sort of way, I thought to myself. Turns out, he never combed his hair and it always fell upon his left temple like a trademark. It gave him something to toss at once in awhile. Really quite sexy, I thought.

He introduced himself simply as a native of Edinburgh, a word only a true Scot can pronounce properly. I tried; he chuckled. There was a round of polite but brief introductions, as one by one they slid off their stools and went away or on to the brightly lit focal spot of the pub—the dart board.

The population at the club, I soon learned, was a heavy assortment of Brits, Aussies, and Scots. Sir Bryn of Edinburgh was the master "offshore investment" guru for the bulk of these mostly overpaid, floating ex-patriots from two separate continents half-worlds apart, denizens devoted to the Queen.

I made small talk with the chap at my left elbow that night, "chatted up" the bartender, who was a fountain of information on anything a homesick *geijin* would ever want: where to go for dance lessons, *ikebana* classes, when Prince Charles was due in town for the Emperor's coronation...and I think he regularly scalped cheap concert tickets to the Harajuku amphitheatres. But his pastie dinners were great, and only the Prime Minister and building inspector knew how he turned out so many fine meals that fast from his wee kitchen behind the bar, too narrow for a grown man's hips surely! All the time, I felt riveting blue eyes following every move I made.

I had my very first pastie, a meat and veggie-filled pastry pocket, served with a heap of mashed potatoes smothered in thick gravy. No salad, as the Brits, unlike the Japanese, aren't big on them. It was not to be my last pastie. That and the excellent fish and chips, served only certain days as the house special, became my mainstay, and I began to feel and sound like a regular, "hitching myself up to the bar" and ordering my own supper. Haggis, the Scottish national dish, was still a long way off in my Tokyo journey, thanks to Sir Bryn.

And soon, I felt like I suddenly had a very secret get-away place in this swollen-belly metropolis of Tokyo, where I could retire to the warm, amniotic fluidity of English jargon once more. It balanced out the sometimes oppressive effect the foreign, Japanese overload had on me. The grating effects the high-pitched, twangy music coming out of loudspeakers posted on telephone poles all over the city, and the rapid speed of a foreign tongue pounding on my eardrums would remind me daily how out of synch I really was in this world. The overload played so heavy on my ears at times, only to be offset by my tiny kitchen radio tuned always to the AFN—Armed Forces Network—where an occasional ball game from home, top of the hour news, or the "Western Hour" music would remind me of my mother tongue. Once in a while, I longed to go to the club just for its own sort of loud but welcome solace and to speak English to another soul.

I went to the TBC quite regularly after that. Marlene and Arty often made plans to hook up with me later in the evening, making us a nice threesome. Arty was terribly handsome; he and Marlene were a fine enviable couple together, and delighted to be in Japan. I must say that the club began to feel like some sort of small, safe social circle to me. Over time, the gents and their wives got used to me. I took up a dare once to play darts and found I was quite good at it. That's all it took; having played sports in my youth, I still had excellent eye-hand coordination, sparked by some feminine adrenalin rush, and I was "spot-on" with my scores. Over two years I mastered darts, which was like dessert on a fish and chips night. And the game broke the ice and justified my crashing the party at the TBC, if only as a loner and "token Yank."

Then, soon after Christmas when Harry, the bartender, had yet to take down the New Years decorations, I arrived late one evening at the pub. I was refreshed and vitalized from a whirlwind trip to Oregon to welcome my two-day old, first grandson, Geoffrey, and host a fine family reunion at my rental home, complete with a Christmas tree I lifted out of the parochial school dumpster on my way through the snow one magic midnight. It was a white Oregon Christmas.

I was volunteering to help Harry take down the holiday decor when I looked around. There sat Sir Bryn in his rain-soaked, tweed suit jacket, hair matted to his forehead. Conspicuous by his absence over the holidays, he was delighted to tell me, a rapt audience of one, how he was just in from the Philippines, and had married off one of his two sons at New Years in a "rather large affair." I had noticed he was "in and out of Tokyo" on a regular basis. Turns out he had offshore offices in Asia, and one in the British Virgin Islands, known as the BVI for those ex-pat clients of his, and also a popular place to divert considerable funds for tax purposes. He still claimed his "wee castle" in Edinburgh as home, but only for family reunions.

He truly adored his children, was rapturous about his only daughter, respected his wife, who had a high level career in education, but he was neither good at being a father nor a husband, and just showed up at family affairs out of courtesy. His life, for all intents and purposes, was financial finagling for others and living out of a suitcase.

He boasted of being a second cousin of Sean Connery, and of knowing *Chronicles* author, C.S. Lewis, from a series of Irish drinking occasions as a young man, although I didn't do the math on their age difference until years later. He would accurately quote some pretty earthy and temporal philosophies over the next two years, so I didn't doubt him for a moment. This scotch-on-the-rocks Scots, soon to become one of my very dearest offshore friends, was indeed a bit of a gypsy rascal, I thought to myself. Yet at the same time he was one of the kindest, soft-hearted, most generous, romantic, and sentimental gentleman I would ever know. That evening, our friendship was sealed with fine malted whiskey on ice, and it was to grow and mellow for the nexty two years.

We left the club together that night and took a fine meal just doors down the alley along the tracks, visiting long into the night about my challenges at TILC. The world of handicapped children and their individual education needs seemed to fascinate him. He was a talker, but indeed an excellent listener, and appeared to take everything to heart

As if shaping itself into a monthly schedule, by March Sir Bryn appeared again one evening sitting at a table off by himself, thoroughly immersed in a thick, investment journal of some sort, and waved me over to join him when I'd gotten my iced pint. He had a look of clear intent and dug in his satchel, and set in front of me a $60 gift-boxed fifth of the finest Glenfiddich Malt Whiskey special reserve single Scotch.

"Young lady, I happen to know you are in financial straits of sorts, what with a daughter in college and such, and I have a business proposition for you. My clientele here is mushrooming and it's necessary I be in Tokyo on a regular basis to firm up my credibility. I'd like to install an answering machine in your apartment to take appointments, and take a night on your sofa monthly so I may deal with my business. And for that I am prepared to pay your entire rent bill."

My head began to spin, before I had even supped. Here I sat down prepared to share with him my joy that the same college daughter was scheduled to arrive soon from Oregon on her spring break for a ten-day holiday, soothing my desperate homesickness. And now I was facing three warm bodies in one small apartment? This just wasn't going to work. A body on the kitchen floor on a blowup bed did not seem fair-share for paying my rent, tantamount to about $800!

But $800 was $800 and I had been propositioned. By an elder Scotsman. And I could see a tremendous opportunity for saving a bundle this spring, just for having him wire an answering machine on my handsome new desk that I'd salvaged from the *gomi-san* and given three coats of gloss black paint.

In the next two weeks before Kari arrived from Oregon, Bryn had the message phone installed, he took a cubicle room downtown, and then was ever-present in capturing Kari's heart and showing her Tokyo. I went to work days and enjoyed the two at night as Sir Bryn and I showed her the time of her life and shared the glitzy sidewalks of Tokyo together.

I took one day off to whisk Kari away to the famed Nikko Shrine, with wisps of snow still on the ground. In the interims, Bryn showed her every Buddhist temple and Shinto shrine, turned her loose on the three-hundred-sixty-degree Yamanote Loop train ride, and pointed out ideal shops for shopping. We took the train to the shore on the weekend and enjoyed the Iwamotos' hospitality in Chiba City. His Scottish presence and humor only added to their delight in making foreigners welcome. He had now become my escort at events, and was thus just a part of Iwamotos' growing "family" of foreigners. In fact, now that they had met my Kari-*chan*, Bryn-*chan* soon pleased them too.

Bryn fairly whirl-winded my daughter to exhaustion with his wide stride, aided by his trademark umbrella; she often came home weary and awed by the sights. And evenings? When I returned home after a day working with Downs Syndrome youth, cerebral palsied young ladies, off-the-wall autistics, and screaming, biting pre-teens with grave learning difficulties, he would simply hand me a scotch-on-the-rocks.

Then we three were whisked off to a noisy spot to dine on the most Japanese of delicacies under the neon umbrella of Tokyo. Bryn, my soft-hearted, most generous new gentleman friend. I knew he had a penchant for gorgeous, freckled redheads like my statuesque Kari, now a junior at Oregon State, but he certainly stepped up to the role of father-to-daughter for those memorable ten days.

Over the next year and a half, if he happened to be in the country, Bryn fell in as my paramour and my escort to school events. We even enjoyed the hospitality of seaside get-aways with wealthy folk from my adult night classes, where I had continued moonlighting evenings that year, to supplant my financial resources. Through those contacts we made several good "couple friends" and had memorable outings around greater Honshu with them all.

He particularly liked the seaside and visiting pubs with these fine people. He was a hiker, had so much energy and zest for life. He was a comedian, and people so enjoyed his wit, wisdom, and storytelling. Some weekends we would just pack a picnic and ride a train to the end of the line, picnic, walk a bit, visit local museums, all to simply escape the urban noise and crowdedness, then return to the belly of the city once more in the evening. Along the way, he picked up several delighted clients at the club, and educators and corporate contacts through me. It seemed to me that the foreign population, once connected, stayed tightly connected. Tokyo was a good place for Bryn after all.

That spring, Bryn became preoccupied shipping his national costume from Scotland, including a questionable *sporran*—the large white pouch of fur worn suspended in front of the kilt—for an event at the Embassy. It got held up at Customs upon entry because of the "fur," which rankled him a bit, but his clothes finally arrived to Tokyo so that we could attend British Ambassador, Sir J. Whitehead and Lady Caroline's *Robert Burns Day Banquet* at the embassy residence.

Lady Caroline sat on my Board of Directors for TILC, and was a frequent visitor to the school where my high-functioning students prepared lunch for the staff on occasion. We welcomed her visits, and she was instrumental in fundraisers for us, particularly the purchase of a much-needed nine-passenger van for field trips.

We four sat on the stage that night in wonderful high back chairs, like royalty, with the Ambassador and Bryn looking splendid in their full regalia, tuxedo with tails, and Bryn in his clan tartan. And I personally enjoyed the abundant flow of alcohol. As the Scotch supply ran down, Sir Whitehead simply excused himself, slipped off to his residence across the garden, and came back with armsfull of yet more fine Scotch from his personal reserve.

There were bagpipes, which I love, and dancing by lads and lassies in full costume of many fine plaids and crinolines and mute black ballet slippers. It became a kaleidoscope of whirling color spread out before us, down below on the hardwood dance floor, edged with tables set with fine linens and laughing Brits having a very fine time.

And then came the piping in of the haggis.

Now haggis, as Bryn explained in a whisper, is the traditional Scottish steamed pudding made of the heart, liver, and other organs of sheep, minced with suet and oatmeal, seasoned and boiled in the stomach of the animal. The hundreds in attendance stood at their tables, and began to sing something appropriate, probably the national anthem of Scotland, I don't remember, in loud and drunken voices. And Bryn was holding me up by my elbow as I could hardly stand alone.

And here it came, steaming down the aisle on the platter. I was not sure I could eat it, learning its origin from my escort, the fountain of knowledge; but I did. And I quite enjoyed the meal.

Sir J. thought it was terribly funny that he'd gotten me drunk, so Bryn danced with his Lady, and Sir J. just chatted on into the evening with me. When I asked Bryn, during a circle dance presented by the male dancers, what a Scotsman wore under the kilt, truly, he turned and replied, "Not a damn thing, my dear."

It was one of the finest Tokyo moments ever.

The party ran well into the night; we enjoyed ourselves long after the trains stopped running.

Kaleidoscopes turned to absolute blurrings for me. We got a cab, checked into a nearby frightfully expensive hotel, slept it off, and stumbled on to Meguro around noon the next day.

My world was shattered less than a month later, creating circumstances that left me scrambling for yet a third apartment, when the TILC Board determined that spring finances merited a drastic cut-back, and I was "outsourced" on very short notice. With that, the "sponsorship" of my wee apartment was being yanked, and I had to turn to the Iwamotos to underwrite a very fine street-level patio DLK (dining/living/kitchen) in the garden community of Musahi-sakai, out east toward Mt. Fuji. All this put me within walking distance of the prestigious British School where I filled in for someone's pregnancy leave teaching polished, precious, and polite kindergartners, entitled children of the corporate and counselor world. I was the token Yank on a British staff.

I lost track of Bryn that spring in that move and my heart ached all summer that I might never see him again. The move from Meguro had been so abrupt, and only God knew what continent he was on at any given time, dodging hurricanes in the Bahamas or tsunamis in East Asia.

Left to his own means and a quick call to Mr. Iwamoto in late October, however, my fine strapping Scotsman found me, and appeared at my door one day mid-week with a two dozen red roses in one hand and my trusty Glenfiddich in the other, relegating me to tears.

We made the most of our few days together and had a joy-filled eight more months together that year. I asked no questions; he told me few lies. And when my eldest daughter, Robyn, visited in the spring, when I knew I would be leaving and heading home for good afterwards, he sought to be there to meet her and show her the same lavish time abroad that he gave Kari, and etch his humor and charm in her heart as well.

The Japanese professionals of my clientele thought nothing of his multi-continental whirlwind life. They never questioned our spontaneous and simple friendship, let alone his unscheduled presence.

They just knew Pah-to was happy.

I certainly never went to Japan with any notion of finding romance. I was focused on getting my daughter through school and plowing my way out of bankruptcy. Bryn's business acumen, his appearance into my life, and his generosity allowed me financial relief that was so unexpected and cherished that I was able to return home after the Gulf War with a sizeable nest egg.

But in the end, I found more than just romance, as I have yet to find in any man such mutual admiration and meeting of minds, of energy and temperaments, of a sense of wonderment and exploration, and a mutually deep and abiding love of Japan and her people as I found in Bryn. There was nothing about him I would have changed—except perhaps the flop of peppered grey hair on his forehead with my temptation to lovingly push it aside.

Did I love him? Yes, deeply—as much because of his largess and wild zest for life as for the gift and privilege of being able to love again. Sir Bryn, my bragadocious Scotsman, forever etched in my and my daughters' memories. Thank you.

Nikko: Suberashii Jinja!

Nikko: Shrine Extraordinary!

Brittle bamboo brooms on the porch floors outside,
like the dusting of a small snare drum,
wakened me from my thoughts.

I had one Gulliver's travel habit that seemed to serve me well. It came not from purpose, but sheer lack of time: I didn't read up on all the "where-to's" and "how-to's" when I wanted to take a trip. I simply got up and went.

And therein lay the wonderful surprises that kept me going. When I heard of a place worth visiting in general, I made it one of my goals but all too often I didn't know what awaited me—like Nikko.

Nikko, nearly two hours on the express train from Tokyo, is listed as another "must see" for even the shortest of visits. Its glory is contained in the magnificent natural mountain setting, rampant, icy rivers slicing through town, cascades, nearby lakes and waterfalls. It is the home of some of the world's most magnificent structures and shrines, foremost being the Toshogu Shrine, tombs of Ieyasu Tokugawa, 1542, founder of the Tokugawa feudal government, and his grandson.

The term "sensory overload" may have been invented with Nikko in mind. It takes a full day to absorb and I have gone back half a dozen times since, sharing this place with my Robyn and Kari, who were both able to visit me in my second and third springtimes. Each time Nikko revealed more and more with the seasons playing an important part of the enjoyment.

Fall, with its mountain colors, was a most splendid time to motor to Nikko. When I took Kari, there in late March, snow was still on the mountains and winter clothes were required. The sky was blue and the air was very, very crisp. She and I discovered that we had this normally tourist-filled place to ourselves on this day in early spring. Traveling by local bus up to the famous Kegon Falls, wild baboons and their babies crawled all over the hoods of cars and waved to us from the shoulder of the spiraling access highway. The nearby mountains, some five to six thousand feet high, still had much snow on them and fed into crystalline beautiful Lake Chuzenji-ko.

Conical Mt. Nantai, boasting 9,328 ft. elevation, completes the breath-taking panorama. (For the sake of reference, Mt. Fuji rises 12,385 ft.) The landscape is worthy of the Tyrolean Alps.

My first time to Nikko, alone, every yen in my slim budget counted. I was given to walking everywhere after coughing up thirty dollars alone for the round trip train fare. And at this sudden elevation and thin air, every step in the small town seemed uphill.

On my way out of the station, hiking up the shady side of the street, I noticed that Nikko streets are barely two tour buses wide.

Private automobiles in an eternal gridlock from the congested Kanto plain fight their way to the limited parking privileges waiting at the top. I was all too happy to be a foot traveler, although repulsed by the auto exhaust.

I was drawn into a pottery and lacquerware shop that had long ago given up ever dusting its wares from all the hopeless traffic soot. Such was its instant and appealing authenticity, like being at my father's woodworking bench.

I quickly spotted a tea pot and two small dishes that I felt I simply had to buy on my way back to the train that night, having learned not to buy and tote all day, but to bookmark my heart's shopping desires.

A lovely woman wrapped them and set them aside for me; somehow I conveyed while paying that she please "hold for me until train time," to whit she sighed at the *geijin's* cleverness. I enjoyed numerous antique shop window displays and treating myself to an iced coffee in a bottle in one of the twenty-four-hour convenience stores that have come to punctuate Japan in every block.

Stopping at the next corner, I saw an extremely high-pitched roof of what appeared to be a mammoth Buddhist temple tucked deep in the trees some three hundred yards away. A sign in Katakana and large arrow was invitation enough for me: must be a tourist site, I thought. It turned out to be a women's retreat center of what religion I do not know. But I slipped off my shoes and mounted steps to a wide wrap-around porch.

A kindly-faced young woman motioned me inside and I fell to my knees just to absorb the splendor and majesty of what I beheld!

This shrine was overloaded with gold, fresh chrysanthemums as big as dinner plates on the altar, incense wafting to the high ceiling, and a multitude of young women were attending to what looked like a project of replacing the *tatami* mat floor. The room resembled an Arthur Murray dance ballroom and could have held three hundred couples! I leaned back almost falling over as I beheld the giant beams that supported the steep roof. I felt dwarfed by the scale of the room. The pillars holding up the beams, the frames for the sliding *shoji* doors, the entry door itself, the altar, and even the gold and purple banners, deeply embossed, padded and quilted, not to mention the cord that rang the temple bell, were of a size like nothing I'd seen so far; I felt Lilliputian in the presence of it all!

It was very relaxing to just kneel and listen to a small group of modestly dressed women chanting at the altar, their voices muted by the size of the room. And off under the eaves, I could see the manicured grounds and in the distance the volcanic foothills of Nikko rising through a late morning haze in those wonderful shades of bluey-green. Brittle bamboo brooms on the porch floors outside, like the dusting of a small snare drum, wakened me from my thoughts.

The real essence of Nikko begins at the top of Main Street, entrance to the Shrine forest, where the crystalline Otani River runs rampant and icy through a canyon. Greeting visitors at the river is the picturesque, —and perhaps most-photographed—glossy-red Shinkyo Sacred Bridge. It is closed off to foot traffic to preserve its historic value; I would see it on calendars and brochures thereafter, second only as a trademark of Japan to Mt. Fuji itself.

I continued my pilgrimage to the great, dark and eerie forest of Cryptomerias, the great Japanese cedar trees. Many steep foot paths traverse into the park, housing dozens of national treasures, one neighboring the other, in a community of shrines, temples, and majestic five-storied pagoda.

This National Park area is heavily punctuated by vast, steep spiraling stairways that transported me from one level and shrine to another, ultimately ending up at the entry gate to the great shrine where demonic-looking Deva kings guard the Toshogu Shrine—all but a hint of things to come.

From that gate, the path veers left into a courtyard of three storehouses, great buildings with colorful relief paintings and carvings depicting elephants and exotic birds. And as I turned to face the sacred stable building, the only unlacquered building on the grounds, various carvings of monkeys caught my eye, leaping off the relief surface.

Second from the left is that famous panel featuring the "see, speak, hear no evil" monkeys, a saying my father had repeated to me thousands of times in my childhood preachings. I was delighted to be here this very moment. I could feel my father smiling down on me, sharing it.

The color and detail of the buildings was truly marvelous, primary and bright and vivid. Sleeping cats over doorways, shrieking birds in half-flight, elephants lumbering, all the animal carvings seemed but a glance away from real and moving. Breathtaking!

But the architectural grandeur of the seventeenth century is no more magnificently played out than in the Yomeimon Gate of the Shrine, Gate of Sunlight, perhaps the most beautiful gate in all of Japan and most elaborately decorated structures on earth. Photos can never do it justice. Only when I drew a breath and cast my eyes on it, would I know why the nickname "Twilight Gate" implies that you could admire it all day until twilight takes over.

I became inebriated with the gilt and lacquer works and intricate carvings, beams atop columns, branching brackets supporting balconies supporting second-story panels, festooned with the mystical flying dragons. Superlatives become insignificant to what your senses are able to absorb. And yet, some two hundred agonizingly steep steps out back in the deeper cedar forest, lie the simple tombs of Tokugawa, resembling a small bronze pagoda.

Visitors spend hours here investigating lesser temples, shrines along the foot paths, museums and botanical gardens. I suspected that one would have to be a real history buff and zealous Buddhist advocate to enjoy all the exhibits and collections of relics. But this is what keeps Rome and Madrid and countless other capitals going too, I reminded myself.

Only a wonderful trip downhill to the station village, braking most of the way, a cold Kirin beer, and some delicious curry rice at a quaint, antiseptic restaurant near the station would help put all this visual overload into proper perspective at the end of a day.

Every trip I took to Nikko was equally rewarding.

The air is always pure and refreshing. Its sensory abundance gave me energy and inspiration to draw upon in the days to come. Nikko is truly an extraordinary destination locale.

~

I see a tree
Half green, half white;
of leaves and blossoms fragrant.
I wonder: What are Her hopes?
Will she full-bloom
And bear fruit?
Or bear
a heart
of sorrow?

O Kanashii: Hiroshima

Hiroshima is a Feeling

...once you have experienced Hiroshima,
are you like the clans...and marked forever?

I had to see Hiroshima. And I had to see it alone.

For me, Hiroshima would be an overwhelming feeling over sense of place. I would return once again before returning to my Oregon home to reaffirm my first reactions, to deepen my emotions, to observe that hallowed place reflected in the eyes of my companions.

But the first time, I had to see it alone.

As was Berlin for me, Hiroshima was a place of silent transparency enveloping my being, robbing me of breath, numbing my senses with suffering awe.

As a "war baby," my recollections of the war were restricted to the stark monochromes on *Life Magazine* pages, and in the fairly harsh, anti-Japanese sentiments echoed in my childhood home. I harbored no feelings on either side of the emotion scale, short of safe and sane.

Hiroshima is, today, a brisk and bustling city of over a million people enjoying much commerce, the presence of a Ford automobile plant, and a continuing inland commercial center. On the weekend I arrived, the abrupt, mountainous, rolling foothills of this city of small islands on the river delta were awash with the many pastels of spring blossoms. The blue sky was dotted with faint marine disturbances of occasional cloud covers, adding humidity to the already intolerable heat. One always wants to carry a *kasa* in Hiroshima; the rains are fickle and frequent friends.

A lovely, covered turn-around greets visitors at the train station, and pedestrians may board any number of rusty old trolleys striking out in different directions to view the city. I traded my usual choice of an "overview" ride and slipped onto the two-car, wooden trolley marked "Atomic Bomb Dome."

Passing through the depths of town, the nearer we got to the harbor and main river tributary, the older and more tattered the buildings became. Back then, forty to forty-five years since being rebuilt, I noticed the faded colors, flaking paint, monotone and lack of luster in these dirty, windswept streets. High buildings seemed to block out the daylight and add to my gathering gloom.

Somewhat reminiscent of my Portland with its heavy Gothic architecture, those reminders soon gave way to an open park as we approached the river bank and the famed Peace Park.

Stepping off onto a narrow meridian, I waited until the trolley lumbered on uphill and over the arched bridge. Obeying the azure blue-green "go" light, I hurried across the street to a small memorial plaque occupying the entry walk to the park. Festooned with white paper cranes of hundred-foot lengths, a simple plaque set in stone read, "Dedicated in 1945 to those who died here..." Camellias opened up their tight faces to me as if to whisper, "There is a springtime of hope here, you know." It was lovely.

On Prefecture soil, I stood at Ground Zero, two feet from the bombed out dome-like shell that has endured worldwide infamy ever since that hallmark day, August 6, 1945, when the first atomic bomb used in warfare was dropped on the center of this peaceful fishing village on the shore of the Inland Sea of western Honshu. Nearly one hundred thousand people lost their lives that week, many more dying from the effects of radiation thereafter.

Now a symbol of the peace movement in the Peace Memorial Park, the shell seemed to irradiate loud yet hollow cries from eternity, from the agonizing pain and throaty utterances from faceless bodies. My mind was convulsed with pictures of the sheer white blast and wind tunnel that followed, decimating countless generations to come of the "what might have been."

My dear friend and Tokyo hairdresser, Arden Yamanaka, spoke, after a year of friendship, in quiet resignation, of his lineage spared only because his grandmother had been off in the foothills, behind the mountains, visiting relatives, and those very mountains served as a shield to the neighboring villagers who came to query the bright light in the sky, and found thousands dying of thirst on the shores of a river running red with blood of many clans.

As I stood overwhelmed by my thoughts, parched dry with emotion, my anger swelled, and in profound grief I wanted to scream.

Every politician, hawk, and war general should walk the cobblestones of modern Hiroshima, spend two days in her museums choked with demographic and stark videos, and be brought back to a reality that there must never be another atomic bomb, so help us, all our gods!

I stared at the Dome, conscious of the soft footsteps I was making today. This place was, in essence, like a public mausoleum, was it not? Did mankind think seven feet of concrete poured over the top of misery could diminish the feeling? Would my feelings ever disappear?

Once you have experienced Hiroshima, will you be like the clans... and marked forever?

I spent the entire afternoon in the park museum, watching the film footage narratives of events leading up to and after the "great white cloud of lightning," the destruction and devastation of Hiroshima and subsequently Nagasaki.

There was noticeable sniffling and weepy eyes exiting the theatre—great unpretentious heaves and sobbings coming from grown men and women from nations all over the world, come here to trace out the cobblestones and the events.

I will be forever haunted by one giant chunk of concrete, leaning against the museum wall—a silhouette of a human being was charred into its very surface.

Before I left, I joined the reverent throngs from busload tours in front of a giant water fountain, surrounded by wreaths and small bouquets of fresh flowers. I gazed with awe at the statue unveiled in 1958 of the tiny girlchild, Sadako, holding a golden crane in her hand, and dedicated to all the children killed by the atom bomb. Now, children of the world honor her memory with thousands of paper cranes, the symbol of her hope, sent fresh daily.

Sadako is immortalized in the popular juvenile fiction book of the same name, by author Eleanor Coerr, read by millions of children, who send crane chains still as the giant brass drums thrum in each new day in the Peace Park.

That day I wanted to believe that the world will never forget what was done here to those hundreds of thousands of innocent victims at ground zero, or the bomb disease that came after, leukemia, felling generations of victims years and years later.

As I write this now and think of having seen Hiroshima and its Dome, I'm reminded of the wish inscribed at the bottom of the statue: "This is our cry, This is our prayer, Peace in the world."

Okutama: Chuo-sen No Shuten

Okutama: Chuo's End-of-the-Line

...the Tama Range takes on a brushed, chalky look,
frequently muted by the evening dinner smoke,
or thunderous mists of a late afternoon shower.

Perhaps the least known—and perhaps the best kept—secrets in all of Japan was, for me, an area northwest of greater Tokyo in the grand Chichibu-Tama National Park. The southern valley running parallel to Chichibu along the Tama River was a regular destination for me when the pressures of my job, the suffocation of the dense population, or the very asphalt and fumes of Tokyo became too stifling for my thirsty lungs. I simply longed for fresh mountain air and the smell of the woods.

A trip here afforded one of the most reasonable daytime getaways, a trip almost through the mists of time. Once, out hiking from train station to station, I rested on a rather tall wall and marveled at its carefully placed river-washed stones. It was as if the wall spoke to me, "Don't you realize that I am nearly four times older *than your entire country*?"

Upper Tama country was the way I wished more of Japan to be, quiet and unspoiled, and so I had to seek it out frequently.

I would board the Chuo Line out of Shinjuku Station and transfer to the Ome Line's rickety green cars at bustling Tachikawa. The Ome Railway has its terminus at Okutama, where tracks literally disappear into the mountains at the site of an immense bauxite mine.

People in sleepy, almost lethargic Okutama acted as if foreigners rarely ever made it up that far. Perhaps folk considered the two and a half hours away from the safety of the city too far for them. For me, the rewards started the moment the train leaped away from the grasp of the Mitaka terminus and huffed and puffed its way into the tranquil foothills of the Tama Range.

The more the little Chuo Line engine "that could" chugged up the blue-green breast of the Mitakesan mountains, the steeper the ascent became. Up the southern flank of the Tama River Gorge it lumbered at an often asthmatic rate that made me want to lean forward to give it all the help I could!

And the more perilous the track route became, often over wooden trestles spanning rushing torrents below, the more breath-taking was the scenery. Steep, ever so steep. At some points, the bed of tracks literally clung to an embankment, with but a bamboo tree between you and a sudden five hundred foot drop!

Here the Tama Range above takes on a brushed, chalky look, frequently muted by the evening dinner smoke, pollution escaping from Tokyo on a gentle east wind, wonderful pockets of morning fog, or thunderous mists of a late afternoon shower. I have seen the mountains in every hue, every time of day, every season, and cannot count the times I rode out just to either escape the pulse of Tokyo, the madding crowds, or the prospect of having an emotional "cardiac arrest."

Whatever my reason, the remedy was so immediate, and the price so cheap.

I went to the mountains, as Walden did to the pond, to rethink my being. I sat on a swinging bridge over the pristine river and watched the fish play with autumn flies. I basked in the breeze to escape the merciless late spring heat of the city. And I donned the layered look of my wools in early autumn to hike the wonderful manicured paths and wonder at the splendor of the explosions of color throughout the hills.

In spring the dogwood, cherries, and plums would wave their fresh blossoms by the hundreds of acres to create an illusion of doves in flight against the hunter green forest backdrop. It's a spring scene no camera can replicate with justice—only in your mind's eye.

Okutama, sleepy one-street village that it is, is not only the hiking gateway to this superb high caves country, but a gateway to numerous spring-fed lakes and well-kept trails throughout the steep gorge. I soon discovered that it rests its reputation on some of the finest fly-fishing and public camping for natives.

Just a three-minute walk from the station is a wildlife and bird museum, truly one of the finest I had ever seen. Unfortunately, it was closed on Monday, which for years was my favorite day off, so it was in my very last spring in Japan that I had the opportunity to finally visit it.

On one special outing, I took my dear friend, Sir Bryn, himself fresh from Edinburgh, to this marvelous museum. We picked up a light lunch at the local mini-mart, where we were literally made to feel like celebrities as we picked out such Japanese delicacies for our picnic as *sushi* rolls, *tsukemono* (pickles), and individual bulbous bottles of *sake* wine. The Japanese seemed to love us when we enjoyed their foods. In the mini-mart we just as easily could have opted for refrigerated enchiladas, Twinkie bars and colas.

We delighted the corner vendor when we bought her luscious strawberries—available year-round in Japan because of intense coastline terrace farming—and some *mikkan* tangerines. We had the definite impression that not too many foreigners made it this far very often, to the end of the Chuo line on the wonderful little engine that could. Yet it will always remain one of my favorite day trips, if only for the unique solitude it afforded.

Bryn and I picnicked around the corner at the nearby Temple grounds near the foot of an ornate bridge leading to a municipal reservoir, famous for its wysteria gardens and open-air picnic kiosks. Here, under ancient cedar trees, the girth of which would seat two dozen campers, we enjoyed our lunch as puffy white clouds gathered rapidly overhead, a hint of a thunderstorm to come.

The paint job on this temple was pitiful and the timbers looked as if they would implode on a very hot day, yet the trees spoke to us in the breeze of wonderful festivals gone by on this very old, sacred ground. And suddenly I liked being in this dark and dusty place under benevolent cedar boughs that also hid us from the scorching sun.

After lunch, inside the sparsely staffed museum, open this day in the afternoon, we were treated to wall-sized maps, photos, taxidermy models of every specie that flies or crawls the forest. Electronic curtains whizzed open to reveal an eighteen-foot square screen as we sat through a breath-taking, twenty-minute slide show traversing the Chichibu glens.

On an eight-speaker sound system, Kitaro's music accompanied the presentation. No voice, thank goodness, just a chance for your senses to be smothered by incredible close-up photography on each millimeter frame—thunderstorms on the mountain crests, downskirts of rain dancing tip toe, fineline feather close ups of nested babies being fed by their parents, deer, fawn, and all the brilliance of dogwood and azalea springs in this pristine forest—a neighboring cousin to the poor, smog-choked Tokyo we had left so far behind us.

As we traveled home that evening, on the last train off the mountain, great rumblings of thunder echoed in the canyon could be heard through our open car windows—exciting springtime music to my ears. And the invigorating smell that follows spring rain filled me with more peace and well-being.

On one of many other occasions to Okutama—I may hold the "Most Frequent Foreigner" award—I found five elderly, stoop-shouldered couples gathered at the same Temple grounds in a hearty game of Japanese style croquet, called "gateball." I marveled at their gnarled hands, hunched bodies, offset by their intense fervor for the game. I suspected they were perhaps permanently disabled from harvesting such gigantic loads of firewood upon their backs, or planting and harvesting the steep, terraced rice paddies visible everywhere the eye could see on the east and west flanks of this canyon.

Time now accorded them the retirement they so richly deserved. Punctuated by their *furoshiki* (cloth-wrapped) picnics, they too would enjoy a long, drawn-out afternoon under the awning of these ancient trees I had grown to love. Japan's white-haired population takes gateball very seriously, as evidenced by the oversized scoreboard leaning sacrilegiously against the altar stairs. With just as much conviction, a scorekeeper would step to the board each time to record the hash mark of a point earned with big, fat chalk. I shall always remember the noisy gusto and childlike pleasure with which they all were enjoying the game, each other, and the moment.

I have bicycled to work through the famed "firefly park" of Chofushi while the dew was still on the morning grass and seen similar teams of elderly couples out in their delightful blue and white sunbonnets having their daily round of competitive fitness games. It's the laughter and camaraderie that accompanies the sport that I found so heart warming. Couples, always couples, drawn together in their golden years for perhaps their first real time of togetherness, enjoy the hearty laughter, far and away from the asphalt work prisons of so many years past.

The patriarchal couples seem to blossom together and exhibit western habits like hand-holding and snuggling on benches. It's as if they finally have time to enjoy family, their grandchildren, and to travel. They represent a significant proportion of the traveling population on excursions, and even to Tokyo's Disneyland.

So as my solitary lunchtime went fairly unnoticed that day, the ballplayers had welcomed the fleeting notoriety of having an audience in me. For this one special weekday, the temple grounds of old Okutama came out of the dust, alive once more. How I wish my ancient cedar tree could talk to me…and tell me more.

~

I am set adrift
On the steel rails of Nihon
Transposed in three hours
Into silence and time.
I see rock walls;
they are ancient.
And gnarled pear trees,
And ninety-seven year
peasants…
Still tilling their fields.

Matsumoto: Dai Na Kuroi Shiro

Matsumoto: Great Black Castle

...taking your breath away with its majesty; like the lone black swan in a flock of white, it is not ugly in its uniqueness.

I have been to the mysterious city of Matsumoto three times, once by myself, once with my friend Jane, once with tourists in the pouring rain. Each visit revealed more of its history and my fascination.

The site of a castle is always thrilling, and Matsumoto's own Black Castle was no exception. I had been to the most impressive castles in Odawara, Osaka, and Kyoto, but I couldn't leave Japan without seeing the magnificent Black Castle, second most famous only to Himeji's "Egret Castle" in the vicinity of Kyoto.

High on the slopes of the Japanese Alps, traveling due west of Tokyo almost four hours by rail, the train ticket was a very expensive $60 to my pocketbook, but not "dear" by Japanese travel standards I am told. Matsumoto and many fine lakes rise up out of a high mountainous basin. All this whirrs by at an unfortunately dizzying rate on the fast trains necessary to get there. The station in Matsumoto is very modern and most impressive as it greets visitors with its blazing neon reader boards that boast its single attraction: the castle.

Somewhat Bavarian in nature but quaint and inviting with traditional winding streets, Matsumoto could be just another lovely town were it not for the great moats and lakes inhabited by wonderful wildlife and black swans. The castle rises dramatically one kilometer north of the station, seemingly out of nowhere—I was almost there before I spotted it. Black, instead of traditional white, with the snowy Alps as a backdrop, it is one of the of many photographic signatures of Japan.

Time and progress have surrounded it with the traditional souvenir shops, a cultural center, and of course a large, two-story folklore museum which seems to always be part of any "National Historic Treasure" all over Japan.

Stepping through the ticket wicket and onto the grounds, faced with a moat that must be sixty feet wide, the elegant six-story feudal structure that dates back to 1504 took my breath away with its majesty. Destroyed repeatedly by fire and rebuilt to its authentic present state, its uniqueness was its own beauty, enhanced by the resident swans that graced its moat.

Rain or shine, or on a particular national holiday when thousands of Japanese flock to town for the traditional Wisteria Festival, dahlia competition, or tea ceremonies, I never tired of the magic of these spacious castle grounds. From atop the six story turret, I could spy on the people below and almost hear the arrows flying in harsh battles for the land. I imagined flaming arrows falling into the magnificent deep moat, now alive with ancient carp of many colors.

One spring day, my chin leaning on a tiny cold window ledge at dizzying heights, I heard the thunder roll across the eastern shoulders of the Alps, rainskirts tickling the slopes surrounding Matsumoto. I daydreamed of lumbering cartwheels carrying supplies to the thousands of *samurai,* held within the keeps of this castle of the sixteenth century, where clans clashed and warriors fell and Japan was in a constant state of flux and feudal uproars.

Somewhere out there in the peaceful and almost idyllic suburbs of whitewashed Matsumoto, maestro Suzuki of music school fame resided and held court weekly on Thursdays for visiting students and their families. I scanned my coin-operated spy glass imagining I was looking right into his orange tree-laden backyard, wishing I had come on a Thursday for such a rare experience. How thrilling to be in the same town as the maestro and know that the gift of his music-learning techniques has given the opportunity for youngsters all over the world to pursue music.

The aura about this alpine town with its crisp, clean air was why I returned often. I loved the cold, rampant river that cut through the city center. Matsumoto's fame for its buckwheat *soba* noodle houses, and their affordable lunches in open-front tavernas were the highlight of my visits. I always came away with a gift box of *mochi*-cakes stuffed with sweet bean paste, just a keepsake to myself, and often bought just for the fine wrappings.

I shall never forget the visit when Jane and I, holding tickets on the last express train to Tokyo on Sunday night, eager for a quick meal before boarding, showed our tickets and timeline to the waitress/shopkeeper as she took our order, hoping she would show us some preference and serve us quickly. She did—a fine shrimp-rice meal with hot *miso* soup and shredded cabbage plate, tea, and a fruit cup.

When the loud speaker in the station announced our train boarding, she swept us out of our booth, shoved us physically through the gate, still in her checkered apron, as she shredded the *kippu* (meal ticket), as if to say, "This meal is on me, foreigners; welcome to Matsumoto, and come again!"

Such was the hospitality I found, past and present...always the very soul of Japan.

Sayonara...Kanashii Wakare

Spring Sayonara Tears

Suddenly, I realized that some day
I might bring my grandchildren here to toss rocks,
and share this great smoky Tama River Valley with them.

Pastor Westby of St. Paul's International Lutheran Church, Chiyoda-Ku, just blocks from the Imperial Palace, counseled me in a very soft voice in his modest first-floor office.

"Going home to be a grandmother is not a very good reason, Patti." Moving on with his wonderful, wry smile and twinkling eyes he said, "They are still at the poopy-pants stage and not that much fun. Why don't you wait until they can hop up in your lap and go camping with you?" He was referring to the three wonderful grandchildren born to my son Bryan and daughter Robyn while I was abroad in what now seemed a very short period of time.

Megan was already a twenty-two-month toddler. I had welcomed Geoffrey and just five months ago had helped name him on my Christmas furlough. And "miracle child," Autumn, weighing in three months early at two pounds-two ounces some fifteen months ago was now a robust and fast-moving toddler also. These grandchildren, whom I hadn't seen much since, precious babes in arms, were irresistible faces shared only in frequent snapshots.

I longed for their warm hugs and devotion.

With my deepest respect for Pastor Westby, nonetheless his words were falling on deaf ears.

I was desperately homesick. And my feet hurt—"foot rot," unbearable, and getting worse with each spring rain. Now early May, the skies were grey flannel and had not parted to make way for the sun in endless weeks. "Rainiest spring in decades," the NHK weatherman would tell me. And at my own half century mark, I was beginning to feel old in a megalopolis surrounded by beer-loving "juppies" who could out-run me at any green light.

I'd gone through three addresses, scores of endearing foreign friends who had come and gone through St. Paul's on their foreign postings. I was becoming one of the old timers here. In just three years, I wasn't sure I could take any more *sayonara* parties and recreate friendship after friendship on this annual basis that seemed to be life in Tokyo for the foreigners.

Fall had always been my personal season of unrest—my favorite time of the year in greeting the colors and welcoming the cooler days and moving somewhere in my life, always the fall. Yet here I was in spring, feeling a real sense of urgency to move on to greater things in my life. It was spring and I was overwhelmed with a great and sudden sadness.

The emotional impact hit me this day with the realization that this would be my last spring on the island of Honshu. I needed to say goodbye to a lifetime passion and end an affair few have the opportunity to enjoy, the love of a land beyond my own Pacific sunset.

To this day, I cannot go to the Oregon Coast to visit my eldest daughter without putting my toes in the sea and remembering the warmth of Kamakura Bay.

I cannot watch the sun go down in the west without recalling a brilliant and searing sun come up out of the east near Nachi Katsurai.

It is with almost physical pain and longing in my heart that I look off to the southwest and think with fondness of the Iwamoto family I left behind—and the timid, sweet sister-like Japanese teacher assistants, Machiko, Miho, or Kumiko, at the prestigious Tokyo British School where I was privileged to teach kindergarten one brief spring.

I remember Pastor Westby and the faces of my exuberant mixed Japanese-American Easter choir at St. Paul's, and I think of dear Yoshi who befriended me, the Hayashi's who watched out for me, and the *tonkatsu* restaurant couple who weekly fed me.

Japan with its mountains and blue seas and tea fields and rice paddies, tile roofs and Shinto priests, lotus ponds, and dank cedar forests held a family to me—dear people who opened their minds and hearts and homes and arms to welcome a poor, slightly bewildered, single foreigner to their beautiful, magical, ancient country

My family walked me over asphalt, sand, and cobbles, and helped me to see behind and beyond Japan's scenic magic into personal relationships welded by the most perfect bonds of human values: honesty, trust, and respect—bonds sealed with food, drink, song, and international languages that know no barriers.

I have refreshed myself from the wellspring of these long and wistful moments ever since.

What began as a single, brief journey and very intimate chapter in my life must go down in my personal history as a three-year love letter.

Japan, I bow to your land of most surprising suns—and sunrises and sunsets—and to every one under them who touched my life in special ways.

And so...

On Monday afternoon, May 19, 1992, I took my favorite orange Chuo Line train and rode slowly up the "think-I-can" grade to Okutama. I crossed the bridge and found the wonderful manicured hiking trail that would meander down river to the village of Ome, where I could cross another fragile foot bridge and board a return train.

Dogwood trees swayed in the evening breeze, holding out their spring flowers like prayerful, supplicating hands outstretched. Evening birds darted and their songs echoed in the canyon. Dusky cooking smoke scented the breeze as it had done for thousands of years—rising in the air like blue incense.

I was reminded once more of the very ancient ground on which I trod. I leaned against a warm boulder for a moment. I crossed the swinging wooden bridge and sat, legs dangling, to watch the fish dart in the shadowed shallows. I heard voices of two young boys pitching rocks below, near a fork in the river. As boys must be doing this very moment all over the world, I thought to myself.

Suddenly, I did not feel so many thousands of miles away from my children and the new grandchildren, still strangers to me.

And just as suddenly, I realized that some day I might bring my grandchildren here to toss rocks, and share this great smoky Tama River Valley with them.

And then it felt right to make plans to say *sayonara* to the land of the "surprising sun" and depart in deepest gratitude for all I had been given in these three remarkable years, and for who I had become in this exotic land. I was returning alone, yes, but no longer *hitoride* in spirit.

Domo arigato, Japan.

Epilogue

Friends are the Laughter
Friends are our life and our love.
Friends are a gift? Yes.

Saying goodbye, with all the parties that attended it, was not a decision made lightly, poopy-pants babies waiting for me or not. Rather, it felt like a deep surface wound across my heart, and there are days I bleed inside with a strange longing for the faces and devoted friends I left behind. The whole experience is so vividly etched in my mind, in color, that often I am given to bursts of tears thinking of isolated events and places, hot tears of longing.

Ending my affair with a country and people who had so embraced me and mine took weeks, as I packed up my Musashino apartment and gave away the bulk of my earthly possessions there. Back into my European cloth backpack and monolithic brown Samsonite luggage I went.

Twenty-three times I had crossed the Pacific Ocean, chasing the sundown or greeting the sunrise. And now I would land in San Francisco on June 26, and in six weeks I would have a job, a house, and bring my trusty VW Fox out of storage and take up where I left off on the Oregon high desert—like I'd never been away nor missed a beat.

August 24 I would return to the classroom once more. Lucky me. Serendipitous.

With a roof over my head, being caregiver for an elderly woman who had known me since I was a new bride, I would repatriate socially into the old circles of dear friends who seemed quite thrilled to have me back. I would welcome my fourth grandchild into my life and hear her first cry, see Kari graduate from the University, and nurture my little nest egg on Wall St. long enough to buy my first home within five years.

Life just seemed to fill up again, gaggles of grandkids and giggles of beloved grown ups. The most difficult thing for me in all these years back, however...

...is going to the Pacific shore,
watching the sunset,
and knowing it is rising
somewhere over Tokyo
on ones I love so much.

I wrote and illustrated this sayonara haiku
for my St. Paul church family at my Sayonara party
hosted by Pastor Carl & Elaine Westby, June 1992 in Tokyo.

Arriving in Tokyo
This woman's been up for 36 hours!

My apartment in Gotanno

Akira and Tsuneko Iwamoto with Patricia

Tsuneko in The Garden

Here are the children!

The wonderful Iniri Kite Festival

The Hayashi clan visit Koya-san.
Naoko, Pat, Prof. Ryoichi, Yoshihiko Akitoshi, Tsnueko

Pah-to on Miyajama

Professor Ryoichi Hayashi welcome dinner

Robyn's spring visit
Patricia, Robyn & Toru's precious wife, Hatsue Yabe

Kari and mom in the tea room